# Stateless

# Attribution

Toward International Accountability in Cyberspace

John S. Davis II
Benjamin Boudreaux
Jonathan William Welburn
Jair Aguirre
Cordaye Ogletree
Geoffrey McGovern
Michael S. Chase

Sponsored by the Microsoft Corporation

For more information on this publication, visit www.rand.org/t/RR2081

**Library of Congress Cataloging-in-Publication Data** is available for this publication.
ISBN: 978-0-8330-9840-5

Published by the RAND Corporation, Santa Monica, Calif.
© Copyright 2017 RAND Corporation
**RAND**® is a registered trademark.

Cover graphic: erhui1979/GettyImages

Limited Print and Electronic Distribution Rights

This document and trademark(s) contained herein are protected by law. This representation of RAND intellectual property is provided for noncommercial use only. Unauthorized posting of this publication online is prohibited. Permission is given to duplicate this document for personal use only, as long as it is unaltered and complete. Permission is required from RAND to reproduce, or reuse in another form, any of its research documents for commercial use. For information on reprint and linking permissions, please visit www.rand.org/pubs/permissions.

The RAND Corporation is a research organization that develops solutions to public policy challenges to help make communities throughout the world safer and more secure, healthier and more prosperous. RAND is nonprofit, nonpartisan, and committed to the public interest.

RAND's publications do not necessarily reflect the opinions of its research clients and sponsors.

Support RAND
Make a tax-deductible charitable contribution at
www.rand.org/giving/contribute

www.rand.org

# Contents

# List of Figures, Tables, and Case Studies

**FIGURES**

**TABLES**

**CASE STUDIES**

# About This Report

The attribution of a malicious cyber incident consists of identifying the responsible party behind the activity. A cyber attribution finding is a necessary prerequisite for holding actors accountable for malicious activity. Recently, several cyber incidents with geopolitical implications and the attribution findings associated with those incidents have received high-profile press coverage. Many segments of the general public disputed and questioned the credibility of the declared attributions. In this report, we review the state of cyber attribution and we consider alternative mechanisms for producing standardized and transparent attribution that may overcome concerns about credibility. In particular, this exploratory work considers the value of an independent, global organization whose mission consists of investigating and publicly attributing major cyber attacks.

The authors would like to thank Herb Lin, Isaac Porche, and Martin Libicki for their formal critiques of an earlier draft of this report. The

## Key Findings

Analysis of recent cases indicates that the practice of attribution has been diffuse and discordant, with no standard methodology used in the investigations to assess evidence, nor a universal confidence metric for reaching a finding.

In several cases, investigations were performed but no formal attribution finding was made public by the investigative entity or victim. Further, public statements of attribution have been met with suspicion, confusion, and a request for greater transparency about the investigation and the evidential basis.

The main challenge in cyber attribution concerns the difficulty of reaching a cyber attribution finding. Technical, political, and all-source indicators are all tools used in determining attribution, and usually are used in some combination.

A second cyber attribution challenge concerns the issue of persuasively communicating a finding to an intended audience. Credibility hinges on several factors: strong evidence, demonstration of the requisite knowledge and skills for reaching a correct conclusion, a track record of accuracy and precision, a reputation for objective and unbiased analysis, and a transparent methodology that includes an independent review process.

Effective cyber attribution investigations will reflect these considerations and achieve credibility in the eyes of the target audience.

analysis also benefited greatly from informal conversations with several researchers and practitioners within the cybersecurity community.

The Microsoft Corporation sponsored this research and asked the RAND Corporation to assess the potential merits and challenges of an organization for performing cyber attribution, and to explore construction of such an organization. The research was conducted within the International Security and Defense Policy Center of the RAND National Security Research Division (NSRD). NSRD conducts research and analysis on defense and national security topics for the U.S. and allied defense, foreign policy, homeland security, and intelligence communities and foundations and other nongovernmental organizations that support defense and national security analysis.

For more information on the RAND Center for International Security and Defense Policy, see www.rand.org/nsrd/ndri/centers/isdp or contact the director (contact information is provided on the web page).

# CHAPTER ONE

# Introduction

There are increasing risks of cybersecurity incidents that have geopolitical implications and that potentially pose threats to safety, security, and economic well-being. Recent notable examples include the attack on the Ukrainian electrical grid (Industrial Control Systems Cyber Emergency Response Team, 2016), the Stuxnet worm unleashed on an Iranian nuclear enrichment facility (Zetter, 2014a), the breach into the U.S. Office of Personnel Management (OPM) that led to the theft of tens of millions of highly sensitive personnel records (Hirschfeld Davis, 2015), and the WannaCry ransomware attack (Perlroth and Sanger, 2017).[1] The perpetrators in each of these cases were linked by a variety of experts to capable state and nonstate actors.

As information technology becomes more widespread and cyberspace more integrated into our daily lives, the likelihood of compromise by malicious actors increases. The U.S. Office of the Director of National Intelligence (DNI) assesses that more than 30 sovereign states are developing offensive cyber-operation programs (U.S. Senate, 2017). Furthermore, these capabilities are increasingly in the hands of criminal and other nonstate actors (Owens, Dam, and Lin, 2009). The spread of offensive cyber capabilities and their increasing commercial availability has the potential to destabilize governments and threaten the Internet technologies on which we are increasingly dependent. In the absence of credible institutional mechanisms to contain hazards in cyberspace, there are risks that an incident could threaten international peace and the global economy.

To promote a stable international order and reduce the risk of conflict stemming from cyber activities, a number of states, nonstate actors, and international institutions have worked toward agreement on the applicability of international law and norms of responsible state behavior in cyberspace. In a 2015 United Nations (UN) Group of Governmental Experts Consensus Report and in the 2015 G20 (Group of 20) Leaders' Communiqué, major cyber powers including Russia, China, and the United States affirmed that international law applies to cyberspace and that states should commit to norms of behavior, including the

**Recent cyber incidents, including the WannaCry attack, indicate the increasing threat posed by malicious state and nonstate actors.**

---

[1] This paper uses the concept of *cyber attack* in a broad and colloquial sense to include intrusions in cyberspace that compromise the confidentiality, integrity, or availability of data. In our usage, cyber attacks include exfiltration and espionage operations as well as destructive or degradative attacks. Other researchers distinguish between cyber attacks and cyber espionage. For instance, see Owens, Dam, and Lin (2009, pp. 1–2).

commitment to refrain from cyber attacks that impair critical infrastructure (G20, undated; UN General Assembly, 2015).[2] Other efforts, such as the *Tallinn Manual* 2.0, have further clarified how international law might apply to state action in cyberspace (Schmitt, 2013).[3] These developments are an important step forward in building shared understanding that will help promote stable relations between states. However, there are no corresponding institutions and processes to encourage states to fulfill their commitments and address grievances when malicious cyber activity occurs. In other spheres of international relations, the global community has undertaken formal treaty commitments—for instance, the Treaty on the Non-Proliferation of Nuclear Weapons and the Chemical Weapons Convention; in addition, mechanisms have been established to monitor and enforce compliance, such as the International Atomic Energy Agency (IAEA) and the Organization for the Prohibition of Chemical Weapons (OPCW). Due to disagreements among states about the value and content of a formal cybersecurity treaty, the technical challenges associated with monitoring cyber activity, and the relative novelty of cyberspace as a domain of offensive operations, there are no widely accepted institutions and processes specifically designed to hold malicious cyber actors accountable for their actions.

Part of the challenge of accountability in cyberspace is the lack of high confidence and publicly persuasive attribution of responsibility for cyber incidents. Cyber attribution requires examining evidence to determine responsibility, analogous to the role of forensics professionals in the criminal justice system. A cyber attribution investigation requires intricate analysis of technical data, an understanding of political or economic motivations, and, if available, analysis of relevant all-source intelligence. Due to the complex technical and multifaceted nature of cyber attribution, specialized and robust capabilities are necessary to undertake an investigation, and even when resources are dedicated, an investigation might not reach a high-confidence and credible finding in a timely fashion. There are an increasing number of government entities, private firms, and research organizations that have the capability to undertake investigations to attribute the source of cyber attacks. However, these entities do not follow a standardized research methodology and employ different naming conventions for cyber threat actors and confidence metrics for their findings, as evidenced by their various attribution reports. When these entities publicly make attribution claims, their findings have sometimes been cast as politically motivated, perceived to be based on limited or opaque evidence, are denied by the accused, and met with skepticism by others. Persuasive attribution is a necessary

---

[2] Note that neither the G20 statement nor the UN Group of Governmental Experts statement includes norms that would prohibit cyber espionage.

[3] The *Tallinn Manual* represents the views of a group of international law experts and is not a legally binding document.

prerequisite for publicly holding malicious actors accountable for their actions. In addition, sharing the details of cyber attack tactics and infrastructure through published attribution findings can assist network defenders in thwarting future attacks. In some cases, attribution might also impose direct costs on actors by "naming and shaming" them. However, it is important to note that attribution alone is not always sufficient for accountability, especially if attackers do not care if they are publicly outed. Although an attribution finding might facilitate effective enforcement mechanisms, it does not always itself produce accountability. Nonetheless, improving publicly persuasive attribution practices will have benefits for cyberspace users at large.

In this paper, we review the current state of cyber attribution, study the factors that hinder the perceived credibility of attribution findings, and consider institutions and processes to overcome the credibility challenges. To accomplish this goal, we reviewed a sample of high-profile cyber incidents through 2017 that involved attacks across national boundaries and we consulted with cybersecurity practitioners and researchers familiar with the process of attribution. We studied these incidents from the perspective of cyber attribution and considered the factors that affected whether an attribution investigation was performed, the kind of organization that performed the investigation, and whether the public statement of an attribution finding was perceived to be credible and persuasive. We considered the existing ways in which attribution investigation entities operate and the potential mechanisms through which informal or formal collaboration might affect the transparency and credibility of cyber attribution findings.

We explore the creation of a standing organization consisting of private-sector and other nonstate actors tasked with attributing major cyber attacks. This organization would have a narrow mandate to attribute responsibility at the highest possible confidence level and greatest degree of precision that the available evidence supports, and to release its evidence and findings to the public. Importantly, it would not undertake enforcement activities. While we briefly discuss the benefits and drawbacks associated with such a formal organization, the focus of this paper is not to demonstrate that our proposal constitutes the single best approach, but to consider its potential merits and challenges, and to explore its construction. To uncover features and functions of a cyber attribution organization, we analyzed relevant intergovernmental organizations, ad hoc investigatory processes, and multistakeholder bodies.

A key element of our recommendation is that a credible and transparent attribution organization should not include the formal representation of states. Our analysis of attribution practices indicates that government officials often publicize attribution claims for political reasons, and when they do, they do not share the evidence for their findings because they are based on sensitive sources and methods. These factors, coupled with the general decline in trust of government globally, have resulted in the perception that government attribution claims lack transparency and credibility. Although some highly capable states possess all-source intelligence capabilities that might be required to support an attribution finding, there are many examples of attribution investigations conducted by the private sector and nongovernment researchers for which specialized intelligence capabilities are not necessary. These examples indicate that government intelligence capabilities are not always necessary for high-confidence attribution. An attribution organization that does not include government-derived sensitive intelligence should not be expected to reach high-confidence attribution in all cases. Indeed, there will likely be a set of cases in which a non–government-aligned attribution organization is ill equipped to produce an attribution decision without the insights that government intelligence agencies may be able to provide. Nevertheless, in cases that will not require intelligence resources, an appropriately structured and governed organization without government membership can undertake more-transparent investigations and may be more readily able to present the evidence for public review. In this way, the organization can promote greater credibility in its attribution findings and enable other actors to undertake additional follow-on enforcement or network defense actions.

In the following chapters, we present a review of notable cyber attacks and a discussion of cyber attribution in practice, with particular attention to achieving credible and transparent attribution. Our discussion is intended as a high-level overview through the use of illustrative examples, rather than as a comprehensive or exhaustive assessment of all facets of this complex and dynamic terrain. We offer several key insights about the dynamics of cyber attribution as currently practiced and consider several mechanisms for how investigative entities can collaborate to perform a cyber attribution investigation. Following our overview of attribution in practice, we turn to our proposal for an independent cyber attribution organization and discuss its core features.

We consider this work to be a preliminary exploration that provides food for thought on how an independent cyber attribution organization could be structured. Key issues, such as funding, are touched on only briefly. Indeed, many organizational and governance details are best left to be decided by members of the organization itself. More importantly, we acknowledge that our proposal is not the only viable structure and there are other approaches to promoting cyber attribution that have merit. We believe our proposal can fit into a set of solutions, including state attribution capabilities, that will enable improved cyber attribution. These caveats notwithstanding, we present several key characteristics that should be taken into consideration if such a body is implemented.

# CHAPTER TWO

# A Review of Notable Cyber Attacks

Cyber incident victims have sought to identify the sources of attacks since the early days of the Internet.[1] In 1986, Cliff Stoll, a system administrator working at Lawrence Berkeley National Laboratory, discovered multiple intrusion and data exfiltration activities in the lab systems. Stoll collaborated with telecommunications firms and law enforcement officials in the United States and West Germany to conduct a months-long technical investigation that resulted in the identification and apprehension of the attackers (Stoll, 2012).

In the 30 years since Stoll's ad hoc investigation, the ability to detect the source of cyber intrusions and prevent them has grown from resting on the perseverance of a dedicated system administrator into a billion-dollar industry (Morgan, 2015). The global cybersecurity market has ushered in advancements in network and device security, threat intelligence, and scalable data collection and analysis. Notably, a growing sector of cybersecurity services firms have emerged—such as FireEye, CrowdStrike, Kaspersky Lab, Novetta, Symantec, and Trend Micro—that provide consulting services, including cyber attribution investigation. States have also sought to improve their cyber attribution capabilities, recognizing that attribution is an essential component of effective deterrence.[2] The maturation of cybersecurity firms, the development of sophisticated methods of attribution, and the increasing complexity of a networked world mirrors the growing scope, threat, and potential harm from cyber incidents.

In this chapter, we set out a sample of such notable incidents, chosen not for representativeness but for the degree of variation that they demonstrate (in terms of victims, scope, method of attack, attacker, and attribution response). What emerges from a review of these cases is a set of varied attribution responses and reporting approaches that further darkens an already shadowy topic.

> A growing number of cybersecurity firms—such as FireEye, CrowdStrike, Kaspersky Lab, and Symantec—conduct cyber attribution investigations.

---

[1] Victim as used here refers to an entity or organization that is the target of a cyber attack.

[2] For instance, the U.S. Department of Defense (DoD) states in its 2015 *DoD Cyber Strategy* that, "On matters of intelligence, attribution, and warning, DoD and the intelligence community have invested significantly in all source collection, analysis, and dissemination capabilities, all of which reduce the anonymity of state and non-state actor activity in cyberspace."

Table 1 depicts a timeline of notable cyber incidents that involve attacks across national borders. We selected this set of attacks for analysis because they have had geopolitical implications, have been widely discussed in the research community and press, and point to useful insights regarding the practice of attribution. The cases include both government and nongovernment victims and led to a range of impacts, such as physical damage, data exfiltration, and financial loss. The cases also include both simple and complex attack methods, with the more advanced attackers often given the moniker of Advanced Persistent Threat (APT).[3] We reviewed these cases from the standpoint of cyber attribution, including the types of evidence that were available, the parties that analyzed the evidence, the characteristics of public statements of attribution findings, and how the alleged attacker and other relevant parties responded. In addition to the summary in Table 1, several of these incidents are discussed in more detail in Case Studies 1–5.

Our analysis of these cases indicates that the practice of attribution has been diffuse and discordant. Across these cases, there was not a standard methodology used in the investigations to assess evidence, nor a universal confidence metric for reaching a finding. Importantly, the cases also illustrate the distinct modes that entities have used to publicly state attribution findings. In several cases, investigations were performed but no formal attribution finding was made public by the investigative entity or victim. For instance, despite a widely held perception that the Chinese government was responsible for the intrusion into OPM, the U.S. government has not publicly accused them of responsibility. In many of these cases, public statements of attribution have been met with suspicion, confusion, and a request for greater transparency about the investigation and the evidential basis.

In the next chapter, we present challenges faced by entities conducting attribution investigations. Although attribution has advanced from a technical standpoint because of the increased maturation of attribution capabilities, there is still an important challenge of explaining a finding and the evidential basis to the public.

---

[3] APT classification indicates a combination of technical sophistication that can make attribution especially challenging and of long-term remote and persistent access methods targeting a specific victim. See National Institute of Standards and Technology (2011).

TABLE 1

## Notable Cyber Attacks and Their Attribution Characteristics

| INCIDENT | YEAR INCIDENT BEGAN | IMPACT | ATTRIBUTION IN THE PUBLIC DOMAIN[a] |
|---|---|---|---|
| Lawrence Berkeley National Laboratory (United States) | 1986 | Intrusion and sensitive data exfiltration[b] | Criminal trial in West Germany, 1990 |
| Titan Rain (United States) | 2003 | Exfiltration of sensitive data from organizations including NASA, Lockheed Martin, Sandia National Laboratories, and the FBI, as well as U.S. and British defense departments[c] | Widely attributed to China by government and private sources in news outlets in 2005; dissent by Chinese state |
| Estonian DDoS (Estonia) | 2007 | Large-scale DDoS attack of Estonian websites in the context of tensions with Russia | Accusations by Estonian government to Russian state actors; Russia blamed attack on pro-Kremlin youth movement—not state-sponsored actors |
| Stuxnet Worm (Iran) | 2010 | Physical damage to Iranian centrifuges; worldwide computer infection | Widely attributed to the United States and Israel; leaks by U.S. officials |
| DDoS attacks on U.S. banks (United States) | 2012 | DDoS attacks on more than 46 major U.S. financial institutions | Widespread perception of Iranian state sponsorship; initial U.S. government leaks and eventual indictment of Iranian state actors in March 2016 |
| Saudi Aramco (Saudi Arabia) | 2012 and 2016 | Wiped or destroyed 35,000 Saudi Aramco computers; similar attack in late 2016 | In 2012, U.S. officials link attack to Iran in news media |
| Associated Press Twitter account (United States) | 2013 | Compromised Associated Press Twitter account and tweeted false news of an attack on the White House, leading to sharp stock market declines | Attack claimed by Syrian Electronic Army |
| White House and State Department (United States) | 2014 | Significant intrusion in unclassified computer systems | Widely attributed to Russia but no official attribution by U.S. government |
| Sony Pictures (United States) | 2014 | Sensitive data stolen and leaked; significant business disruption | Attributed to North Korean state actors by U.S. President in December 2014 and to Lazarus by Operation Blockbuster in 2016[d] |
| GitHub (United States) | 2015 | Large and persistent DDoS attack on software development collaboration site | Widely attributed to Chinese state actors by private firms and researchers |
| TV5Monde (France) | 2015 | 18-hour TV network outage; false flag leads to false attribution to ISIS[e] | FireEye attributed to Russian hacking group APT28 in June 2015 |
| OPM (United States) | 2015 | Exfiltration of 21.5 million personnel records of U.S. government employees | Widely attributed to China although never officially attributed by U.S. government |

TABLE 1—CONTINUED

| INCIDENT | YEAR INCIDENT BEGAN | IMPACT | ATTRIBUTION IN THE PUBLIC DOMAIN[a] |
|---|---|---|---|
| German Parliament (Germany) | 2015 | Exfiltration and release of 2,420 sensitive files belonging to German Christian Democratic Union | BfV attribution to APT28 in news outlets in May 2016[f] |
| Ukraine power grid (Ukraine) | 2016 | Loss of power for several hours across regional power distribution plants, affecting 225,000 customers | Ukrainian officials accused Russia; private firms suggest possible state actors and/or cyber criminals |
| Democratic National Committee (DNC) (United States) | 2016 | Exfiltration and release of DNC and campaign documents; interference with 2016 U.S. presidential election | CrowdStrike (June 2016) and DNI report (January 2017) attributed to Russian state actors[g] |
| Bangladesh Central Bank (Bangladesh) | 2016 | Successful bank heist of $81 million from Bangladesh Central Bank account at the Federal Reserve Bank of New York using Society for Worldwide Interbank Financial Telecommunication (SWIFT) banking system | Symantec report links to Lazarus May 2016; U.S. intelligence agencies report link to North Korea state news outlets in March 2017 |
| Mossack Fonseca (Panama) | 2016 | 11.5 million leaked documents representing more than 214,488 "offshore entities," leading to numerous tax evasion and corruption charges | No attribution to date; possible hacktivists and/or insiders |
| Dyn (United States) | 2016 | DDoS attack using a botnet of Internet of Things devices against Dyn, a domain name system (DNS) provider, disabling a significant number of websites | No official attribution; widely believed to be a hacktivist organization such as Anonymous, New World Hackers, or SpainSquad |
| WannaCry (Worldwide) | 2017 | Ransomware attack affecting health care, transportation, and telecommunications infrastructure worldwide | No official attribution; some private firms suggest links to Lazarus Group; Russia blamed the United States for creating exploit that enables WannaCry |

NOTE: All information is open-source and gathered from publicly available and widely distributed news outlets unless otherwise noted.

[a] Attribution to an individual, group, or state made publicly available through official reports, news media, and public statements. Attributions can be published by private firms, governments (formal public attribution statements either through an official report, indictment, or an official statement by government officials to an individual, group, or state), or news media citing unofficial and official sources.

[b] Stoll, 2012.

[c] Thornburgh, 2005; Norton-Taylor, 2007.

[d] Novetta Threat Research Group, 2016.

[e] The organization's name transliterates from Arabic as *al-Dawlah al-Islamiyah fi al-ʿIraq wa al-Sham* (abbreviated as Daʾish or DAESH). In the West, it is commonly referred to as the Islamic State of Iraq and the Levant (ISIL), the Islamic State of Iraq and Syria, the Islamic State of Iraq and the Sham (both abbreviated as ISIS), or simply as the Islamic State (IS). Arguments abound as to which is the most accurate translation, but here we refer to the group as ISIS.

[f] The Federal Office for the Protection of the Constitution (Bundesamt für Verfassungsschutz, abbreviated BfV) is a German government domestic intelligence agency.

[g] DNI, 2017.

# CHAPTER THREE

# Cyber Attribution in Practice

The so-called cyber attribution challenge is regularly noted in academic, think-tank, and policy circles as a serious obstacle for promoting cybersecurity. This chapter seeks to provide a high-level overview and advance these discussions by distinguishing two distinct types of attribution challenges. First, there is the oft-discussed challenge of accessing, interpreting, and comparing technical and other evidence in an effort to reach a high-confidence attribution finding in a timely manner. Second, there is an additional challenge of persuasively communicating an attribution finding to a target audience or the general public. We will review each of these challenges in turn, and then describe several key insights to help address the two challenges.

## Reaching a Cyber Attribution Finding

The first challenge concerns the difficulty of reaching a cyber attribution finding. The cyber attribution process involves the identification of the set of machines that enabled intrusion into a victim's computer systems, the identification of a perpetrator that set the intrusion into motion, and/or the identification of an adversary that is ultimately responsible for the malicious incident (Lin, 2016). Although well-trodden territory, it is worth briefly reviewing some of the features of cyberspace that complicate the ability to perform cyber attribution. After reviewing these features, we describe the indicators and evidence used by investigators to assess responsibility.

To begin, cyberspace enables actors to operate with various degrees of anonymity. Malicious actors can intrude on networks and even deliver effects that can go undetected for weeks, if not years. Second, cyber attacks may operate on spatial scales ranging from local targets in close physical proximity with an attacker's hardware to global targets connected by telecommunications technology over great distances (see Owens, Dam, and Lin, 2009). As a result, an attacker, who could be literally anyone in the world, can route attacks through compromised innocent third parties and obfuscate their origin. Third, the evidence that a malicious actor is responsible for a cyber attack is potentially very different than evidence used to attribute other types of incidents. Traditional evidence

> There are several challenges with cyber attribution, including persuasively communicating findings to the general public.

used in U.S. courts often relies on physical evidence that can be observed and recorded (consider the trajectory of a missile or the bullet casings from a gun). In contrast, a passerby would not be able to distinguish between benign code for quantitative research and malicious code for data exfiltration. In addition, traditional legal cases are frequently based on identifiers that are static and are globally unique or at least rarely (if ever) repeated, such as fingerprints or DNA. Conversely, the Internet has a decentralized, dynamic, and open architecture that enables an offender to easily hide his or her tracks by disconnecting devices, changing Internet Protocol (IP) addresses, or leveraging the tactics, techniques, and procedures (TTP) developed by other malicious actors. So, even identifying the specific machines and methods involved in the attack does not guarantee a finding of responsibility.

Relatedly, there are basic questions about the concept of responsibility for a malicious cyber incident. In order to attribute a cyber attack to a given state, it is not sufficient to simply trace the attack to computers within that state's borders. For instance, the cyber attack on DNS provider Dyn involved compromised systems from "millions of IPs across all geographies" (Hilton, 2016). Further complicating the issue, there are varying degrees of complicity when considering possible state sponsorship of cyber attacks. For example, how should an attribution declaration be worded if a nation's leadership only implicitly encourages a cyber attack or knows it is happening but looks away?[1] Even if one identifies the persons involved in the attack, the relationship between the person or persons and host country may be murky.

Attribution in cyberspace involves examining and interpreting hard-to-compare evidence, including technical forensic information, political motives, and all-source intelligence. As a result of the interpretive difficulties associated with attributing a cyber attack, the investigative process has been described to be as much an art as a science (Rid and Buchanan, 2015). Indeed, one expert asserts that multisourced cyber attribution is based on "judgment," as opposed to being a conclusion that can be definitively proved (Lin, 2012). Nevertheless, there are common practices and tradecraft that are used by a variety of experts in cyber forensics that shed light on attribution. While few clues can guarantee a high-confidence finding, there are several factors that provide a basis for an assessment of responsibility.

## Technical Indicators

The tradecraft employed by an attacker and the artifacts of the attack include several technical elements that can be used to support a claim of attribution (Bartholomew and Guerrero-Saade, 2016; DeCianno, 2014). These technical elements can be derived through such forensic

---

[1] For more on the "spectrum of state responsibility," see Healey (2011).

activities as network analysis and inspection of log files, software programs, and executing processes on the victim's computer systems, and of the networks used by the victim through third-party service providers. The elements include text strings, timestamps, command and control (C2) infrastructure, malware samples, and such identifiers as passwords and IP addresses.

Text strings discovered in an attack may include written language that implicates a given attacker. For example, the Stuxnet worm included the string "myrtus," which some experts believe implicated the Israelis based on biblical references (although others argued that the string was simply an acronym related to "my remote terminal units").[2] Implicating text strings may also include the names of the software functions that are found in malicious code. For example, the "wipe-out" function found in malware associated with the Bangladesh bank attack (Case Study 1, below) was linked to malware found in other attacks, such as the Sony attack (Shevchenko and Nish, 2016).

Metadata, such as timestamps, may indicate the time when malware was compiled, the time of infection, and the regularity of the attacker's

---

[2] For example, attackers may leave personal identifiers in malicious code or prevent infections by checking for text strings in registry keys. See Markoff and Sanger (2010).

CASE STUDY 1
## A Cyber Heist at the Bangladesh Central Bank

In February 2016, a hack compromised the international banking system in an effort to steal $951 million from the Bangladesh Central Bank. The hack gave false instructions to withdraw funds from the Bangladesh Central Bank's account at the Federal Reserve Bank of New York (NY Fed) using the SWIFT banking network to complete the transfer (Zetter, 2016). The hack succeeded in withdrawing $101 million before it was stopped by the NY Fed. Of the $101 million, $20 million was diverted to Sri Lanka and later recovered, while the remaining $81 million was diverted to the Philippines, most of which remains lost. The apparent financial motive for the attack led many to suspect nonstate criminal groups, while the Bangladesh government itself accused a range of state and nonstate actors. By mid-2016, private-sector investigators noted that at least three actors had compromised the Central Bank, one of whom used malware associated with the Lazarus group (discussed in detail in Case Study 5). In March 2017, a year after the attack, U.S. intelligence officials corroborated those reports by suggesting North Korean involvement but have not provided any evidence (Symantec Security Response, 2016; Lema, 2017; Groll, 2017).

work schedule. In addition, timestamps may link attacks together. For example, there were identical timestamps associated with code in the DNC attacks and several other attacks of diplomatic organizations (Buratowski, 2016).

Attackers use C2 infrastructure to deliver malware and maintain control of it after delivery. In the case of the Sony Pictures attack, the C2 infrastructure included unaffiliated, compromised hosts, such as mail, gaming, and educational institutions in the United States, Taiwan, Indonesia, India, and China. The C2 software for the Sony Pictures attack also leveraged "sloppy" use of IP addresses linked to North Korean businesses (Sanger and Fackler, 2015).

Nevertheless, the availability of incriminating technical data is no guarantee. Sophisticated adversaries that want to avoid attribution will carefully dedicate resources to deploy false indicators and cast suspicion on other parties (Bartholomew and Guerrero-Saade, 2016). For example, the Russian-speaking actor associated with the Cloud Atlas APT used a document written on a native Spanish-speaker's computer and incorporated Arabic strings, Hindi characters, and rotated IP addresses—probably to complicate attribution (Fagerland and Grange, 2015). It is conceivable that each of the technical indicators utilized in attribution—timestamps, strings, code reuse, etc.—could be manipulated in a similar way to delay or completely avert attribution. Indeed, if some specific technical indicator is deemed to be the most important evidence for attribution (e.g., the closest cyberspace equivalent of DNA), then sophisticated actors will dedicate resources to disguising or false-flagging that specific indicator.

## Political Indicators

A second type of indicator that can assist in an attribution investigation is the political context in which an incident takes place and the relevant motives of capable parties. If a specific actor stands to benefit from an attack for political, economic, or other reasons, then this might factor into an attribution judgment. Similarly, the type of target selected and the specialized knowledge required to exploit that target might also serve as relevant political indicators.

For example, the United States and Israel were widely implicated in the press for the Stuxnet attack on an Iranian nuclear enrichment facility for several reasons. First, the attack used a vast array of technical resources, including the use of multiple zero-days, which only the most sophisticated actors would possess. Political motives served as an additional indicator because degrading the Iranian nuclear program would be beneficial to U.S. and Israeli interests. Similarly, Russia was widely blamed by the Ukrainian government and media for the attack on the Ukrainian power grid due to the selected target, specialized knowledge required for the intrusion, and clear political motives of Russian state actors. The rampant speculation that the Chinese conducted the OPM attack is also partially based on the claim that the Chinese government has an active interest in exfiltrating that type of intelligence from U.S. targets. The attribution to Iran of the Shamoon attack on Saudi Aramco might also be justified in part by an assessment of the political motives of the Iranian regime.

Just as technical indicators are not always sufficient for high-confidence attribution, political indicators also might not be definitive. An adversary might have reason to execute an attack even if how they stand to benefit is not clear on the surface. For instance, the attack on TV5Monde was initially thought to be perpetrated by ISIS, not only because of the false technical flags, but also because targeting a major western news station seemed to be an action that was aligned with ISIS's motives to produce fear and instability in European cities (Case Study 2, below). However, despite the initial assessment, several private firms and French authorities later attributed the attack to "APT28" actors linked to the Russian government (Wilson, 2015). In the case of the financial theft from the Bangladesh Central Bank, a variety of criminal groups—or even states such as North Korea—had motives to undertake the operation.

---

CASE STUDY 2
## The False Flag at TV5Monde

On April 8, 2015, the networks of TV5Monde, a global French-language television network, were hacked, resulting in an 18-hour network-wide outage (Corera, 2016). At the same time, the hackers also attacked TV5Monde social media accounts, posting pro-ISIS propaganda and replacing their profile images with a black screen reading "CYBERCALIPHATE" and "Je suIS IS." The images turned the words "Je suis Charlie," used to convey unity following the 2015 terrorist attacks, against the French public, making the attack appear to be a new ISIS approach. As a result, the attack was immediately and widely attributed to the "Cyber Caliphate" and led to fears of ISIS's cyber capabilities.

However, it later became apparent that the cyber caliphate was just a false flag used in a complex attack with obscure objectives. In the months following the initial speculation, investigations led by the National Cybersecurity Agency of France (ANSSI) and FireEye began pointing to a different source. By June 2015, FireEye reported that their analysis traced the attack to Russian APT28—based on a review of technical indicators including infrastructure, malware, and timestamps involved in the attack (Leyden, 2015; Paganini, 2015).

## All-Source Intelligence Indicators

Intelligence capabilities can also provide valuable evidence for attribution. All-source intelligence includes, but is not limited to, signals intelligence (SIGINT), human intelligence (HUMINT), and open-source intelligence (OSINT). These capabilities may not be widespread globally, and very few countries are thought to possess sophisticated all-source capabilities. With a few notable exceptions, these capabilities and the information derived from them are not readily shared.[3]

SIGINT is intelligence that is produced by collecting and analyzing signals and data from communication and information technology systems (National Security Agency, 2016). If these types of data are available to cyber researchers, they can be especially valuable because they can provide insight into not only the actions of the cyber attackers, but also their intentions. For example, if a government has a signals collection capability on networks that were used in the attack, that government could examine the associated traffic to help discover the source of the attack. If the attacker(s) are also communicating on the same networks, that government could also presumably gain insight into the attack by examining communications about the attack that may give clues as to the source.

HUMINT is intelligence that is produced by collecting and analyzing information from people. In a cyber attack scenario, a HUMINT collector might elicit information from persons he or she thinks could provide useful information about the attack. For example, if a HUMINT collector has access to a source in a government that he or she suspects is responsible for a cyber attack, the HUMINT collector could lead the source to divulge knowledge about the attack or to find out more information to support attribution.

The quantity and quality of data that can be collected by some states with sophisticated intelligence capabilities is greater than that of private firms. However, it is important to note that private firms might possess the ability to collect similar information in the course of business. In fact, a private firm that does business globally could have access to a wider variety of data and people than a "lower-tier" government with very weak intelligence capabilities.[4] In a 2014 report, for example, the independent software testing organization AV Comparatives found that some popular antivirus companies collect

---

[3] The 5-Eyes—an intelligence-sharing relationship that includes the United States, Canada, the United Kingdom, New Zealand, and Australia—is one notable exception. For more, see Farrell (2015).

[4] The Defense Science Board defines six tiers to represent increasing capability to utilize cyber offensive measures and intelligence resources to engage in offensive operations. Our comments about private-sector capabilities compared with intelligence are directed toward lower-tier countries that have limited capabilities. See Defense Science Board (2013).

host, network, software, and file-related data, even when the files are not malicious (AV Comparatives, 2014). The data collected by these antivirus firms may resemble data targeted by intelligence organizations. Such private-sector entities as Internet service providers, telecommunications firms, and social media companies might also be in a privileged position for accessing and sharing valuable all-source evidence. In 2015, Facebook launched a platform that welcomed "credible companies" to contribute high-confidence data on threats discovered in their networks. As of November 2016, the platform had more than 450 participating members. In response to demand, such companies as AlienVault and Soltra have launched similar threat-exchange platforms.[5] Indeed, in cases where a government must fill intelligence gaps, it may need to turn to the private sector for data either through voluntary collaboration or by compelling firms to provide them.[6]

Whereas SIGINT and HUMINT encompass information that is often closely held, OSINT is intelligence that is produced and analyzed by collecting and processing information from openly available sources, such as the Internet. As with SIGINT and HUMINT, OSINT collection and analysis techniques can support attribution. Researchers can analyze social media posts, surf cyber crime–related DarkNet sites,[7] and query Internet resource services, such as WHOIS,[8] to build attacker profiles and to discover bits of information that assist an investigation. Data related to cyber attacks might also be already aggregated and parsed by other organizations and published openly. For example, the publicly available search engine Shodan recently announced a feature allowing researchers to discover malware servers.[9] If private firms can successfully collect and exploit open-source information and enhance their intelligence with the data from the networks, devices, and organizations they service, they might have greater capabilities than some states to effectively analyze potential evidence.

## Linking Indicators Together

A cyber attribution investigation will need to interpret, assess, and weigh all the available evidence. Investigators will also need to link indicators across incidents. Cyber assailants reuse code and infrastructure from one attack to the next. In the case of C2 infrastructure, this means that common software components, such as remote-access tools,

---

[5] See, for example, "ThreatExchange Documentation" (undated), Kennedy (2016), "AlienVault Ossim" (undated), and Soltra (undated).

[6] The FISA (Foreign Intelligence Surveillance Act) Amendments Act of 2008 in the United States is one such example (U.S. House of Representatives, 2008).

[7] For more information on the DarkNet, see FBI (2016).

[8] WHOIS is a system that provides information on domain names and IP addresses (Internet Corporation for Assigned Names and Numbers [ICANN], undated).

[9] Shodan is a search engine for Internet-connected devices. See Shodan (undated).

will be used to maintain persistent connections across different targets. Variants of the BlackEnergy Trojan have been discovered in diverse attacks in multiple countries since 2008 (Baumgartner and Garnaeva, 2014; GReAT, 2016). Software reuse also means that strings, time-stamps, and other identifiers that one would expect to be unique will show up in multiple attacks and serve as evidence that the attacks are from the same adversary. Following the 2016 attack on the Bangladesh Central Bank, Symantec and Kaspersky Lab researchers found code reuse linking it to the activities of the Lazarus group (GReAT, 2017). Investigations by Novetta have connected the Lazarus group to numerous attacks in the United States and South Korea (most notably the Sony Pictures attack) through common linkages such as code reuse (Novetta Threat Research Group, 2016). Furthermore, the Bangladesh attack involved several strings with typos—i.e., "foundation" written as "fandation" and "already" written as "alreay" ("Spelling Mistake Prevented Hackers Taking $1Bn in Bank Heist," 2016); if these same idiosyncratic typos were present in the software of another attack, it would serve as additional evidence of a linked attack.

However, as we have noted, technical indicators can be falsified. So it is crucial that, in addition to linking technical indicators across incidents, attribution investigations need to link the technical indicators with political indicators and other all-source information. A well-founded attribution judgment needs to be based on a holistic assessment of all evidence available. This aspect of attribution might complicate investigations—the experts that are able to assess technical indicators might not be experts in assessing political indicators, while few political experts have much understanding of technical forensics. These distinct types of indicators might seem incommensurate, and there may be challenges associated with reconciling the evidence when indicators point in different directions.

This discussion of indicators highlights the first type of attribution challenge and how attribution investigators have sought to overcome it. We turn now to a second attribution challenge.

## Communicating a Cyber Attribution Finding

A second cyber attribution challenge concerns the issue of persuasively communicating a finding to an intended audience. This challenge is increasingly important for state and nonstate attribution investigators who seek to hold malicious actors accountable for their actions. In this section, we raise some elements related to credible communication to discuss the shape of the challenge, and will return to these themes subsequently.

The purpose of publicly communicating the results of a cyberattack investigation is to inform the public of the identity and methods behind the attack. However, publicly announcing such information may stem from other motives and consequences. For instance, a public attribution statement may encourage victims or other vulnerable populations to bolster network defenses. It may also be used to warn a perpetrator that a response is imminent or to persuade a set of third-party actors to generate support for sanctions. In other cases, the public statement will provide insight and awareness that might call public attention to malicious activity but will not be acted upon otherwise (Edwards et al., 2017). One analogy is of a prosecutor laying out evidence in court to persuade a jury that someone violated the law. For a U.S. court, persuasive attribution may result in a jury conviction followed by sentencing and the enforcement of a punishment, though these subsequent actions (e.g., sentencing or punishment) will not necessarily occur.

In order to be effective, a public statement needs to be credible. An attribution process that lacks credibility may fail to accomplish any of the direct or indirect purposes set out above. Returning to the court of law analogy, attribution that lacks credibility may fail to result in a jury decision that is consistent with actual events and legal standards, even though accurate evidence was presented to the jurors. For example, inept handling of evidence, a failure to present the evidence clearly, or any apparent subjective bias may result in a perceived lack of credibility.

Credibility is established via several factors. Perhaps the most obvious factor is the presence of strong, clear evidence that corroborates an explanation for a given finding. If other independent experts can review, assess, and vouch for the strength of the evidence, this will help to make evidence compelling. More generally, separate from specific evidence tied to particular incidents, there is a set of factors associated with the entity performing the investigation. These factors include demonstration of the requisite knowledge and skills for reaching a correct conclusion, a track record of accuracy and precision in past investigations, a reputation for objective and unbiased analysis, and a transparent methodology that includes an independent review process. Effective cyber attribution findings will reflect these considerations and achieve credibility in the eyes of the target audience.

### Modes of Communicating a Finding

Cyber attack investigations and attributions employ a variety of approaches to publicly communicate their findings and analysis. These approaches vary in mode, detail, and timing. We review a few of the different approaches that have been used to publicly attribute attacks.

Government attributions have varied significantly in form. For example, in the cases of the Sony Pictures, Ukraine Power Grid, and

German Bundestag attacks, official high-level public statements were used to communicate attribution to the public. In other cases, official reports have been published. For instance, following the DNC attack, the DNI published an official report attributing the attack (DNI, 2017), and the U.S. Department of Homeland Security and the FBI released the GRIZZLY STEPPE report (2016), including technical details about the attack (see Case Study 4, p. 34). Furthermore, in additional cases (e.g., the FBI indictment of Iranian state actors for the DDoS attack on U.S. financial institutions) government attributions have come as official actions of retribution.

However, in other cases, government attributions have not come in the form of official, on-the-record statements. For example, government officials have used unofficial and off-the-record communications with news outlets—e.g., media attribution of the Bangladesh Central Bank attack to North Korea citing FBI officials (Finkle, 2017)—to convey attributions. In other cases, such as in the case of attacks against the State Department and the White House and Stuxnet, government leaks have revealed unofficial attributions to the public (Groll, 2016).

Attribution statements by the private sector and independent researchers have also come in different forms. In the case of CrowdStrike's analysis regarding the DNC attack and Mandiant's report regarding APT1, official reports were published. Investigative journalists, notably David Sanger of the *New York Times*' investigation and attribution of the Stuxnet attack, have led to published attribution findings in the public domain that pull from independent research and off-the-record conversations. However, independent researchers have also presented attribution findings and evidence in a variety of other informal ways, including through blogs and social media posts. In this way, attributions have been made through connections in published reports and informal research. For example, while the Operation Blockbuster report on the Sony Pictures attack done by a collaboration of private-sector firms led by Novetta connected the attack to Lazarus, less-formal reports connected Lazarus to North Korea. The same type of informal linkage was used following the Bangladesh Central Bank attack, when an official Symantec blog post (2016) connected the attack to Lazarus (and therefore North Korea).

Although the reasons for different modes of communication and the degree of underlying confidence associated with each are uncertain, the use of different modes of communication has implications for public confidence in attribution decisions.

## Key Insights About Cyber Attribution

From the review of the cases above, we derive several insights about the cyber attribution status quo. The private sector plays a critical role in investigating incidents and making judgments of attribution. However, private-sector entities have their own independent financial incentives to produce high-profile attribution reports. Even when firms share a common goal in identifying and mitigating threats, they do not share frameworks that are easy to compare, resulting in inconsistencies, such as varying nomenclatures. The few governments with attribution capabilities also employ their own opaque research frameworks. In the rare occurrences that governments publicly make cyber attribution claims, their statements are often seen as purely political. And since they do not often formally share the details of the investigation that led them to their conclusions, their conclusions can be easily doubted. Finally, the current fractured landscape of cybersecurity research is not particularly welcoming for victims of cyber attacks. Victims of major attacks do not always seek external support immediately after the incident, because many of these victims either cannot afford cyber attribution assistance or do not know where to turn for help. This reticence may be compounded in the absence of an independent organization that strives for consensus opinion across multiple firms and methodologies.

## A Campaign Approach Is Necessary

As illustrated previously, the infrastructure and exploits that are leveraged in attacks are frequently reused, which enables investigators to link different incidents to the same actors. In other words, past investigations affect current attribution assessments, and attribution investigations must track actors over the course of their varied activity, potentially over years. This means that an attribution investigator must take a sustained "campaign" approach to their investigations, in which multiple cyber incidents are considered in the process of identifying the responsible party. Although sophisticated actors will take pains to change their exploit methods and techniques to avoid detection, this will not always be possible and will increase the costs of conducting attacks. Given the importance of a campaign approach, there is value to standing attribution entities that maintain a shared and easily updated database, rather than independent investigators coalescing in ad hoc cases.

The necessity of a campaign approach will also influence how an attribution organization manages information related to attacks over time. In particular, an attribution organization will need to create a formal nomenclature system so that the attacks can be universally referenced in future investigations. In addition, the characterization of cyber attacks may benefit from a formal approach to describing attacks in terms of exploitation type and severity, among other characteristics; for example, consistent severity characterizations may be useful should a separate body be tasked with recommending punitive actions against responsible parties.

## Fragmentation Among Researchers Can Create Confusion

Collaboration and knowledge-sharing between cybersecurity researchers has increased, but is not the standard mode of operations yet. The lack of a shared knowledge base has created inconsistencies in the investigation approaches and methods of different firms. For example, Kaspersky Lab noted that analysis done by BAE and Anomali on the link between the North Korean–associated Lazarus Group and the Bangladesh bank heist narrowly focused only on "wiper" tool code. Similarly, Kaspersky noted that Symantec implicated the Lazarus Group by identifying malware string reuse in a Polish financial sector attack (GReAT, 2017). Examples such as this make clear that the existing body of research is not consistent in identifying these actors and their TTP because the research was carried out by multiple organizations, each with varying levels of access to critical data and expertise, and sometimes with years-long gaps between assessments. Thus, a shared body of cybersecurity research tools and methods could be useful in future investigations, especially in cases involving cyber actors who carry out regular attacks.

Private firms have their own economic interests in investigating incidents and attributing attacks, and there are incentives to publish findings as quickly as possible and in a high-profile manner as marketing for future clients. Other competing firms might have motives to reject their competitor's findings and point to alternative hypotheses. Without a standardized methodology, or even an industrywide commitment to adhere to rigorous methodology that includes independent review, this might result in a confusing picture for nonexpert audiences.

Further complicating the fragmented nature of the current body of knowledge, private-sector firms and government intelligence agencies separately name the cyber threats they research, leading to divergent nomenclature for common APTs. Figure 1 displays the divergent naming conventions currently used for two major APTs. For example, the APT associated by some researchers with Russia's main intelligence agency (GRU) is known as Sofacy by Kaspersky, as APT28 by FireEye, STRONTIUM by Microsoft, and FANCY BEAR by CrowdStrike. A different APT associated by some with Russia's federal security service (FSB) is labeled APT29 by FireEye, but is known as CozyDuke by F-Secure, and as COZY BEAR by CrowdStrike. The joint analysis report, *GRIZZLY STEPPE—Russian Malicious Cyber Activity* (U.S. Department of Homeland Security and FBI, 2016), lists nearly 50 alternate names for reported Russian military and civilian intelligence services. The Venn diagrams with partially overlapping sets in Figure 1 are intended to indicate that multiple APT names may be based on similar but not identical indicators. Even if these naming conventions have some overlap, they can lead to confusion among politicians, policy analysts, and a public at large already faced with the difficulty of interpreting the results of a technically complex attribution process.

FIGURE 1

## Various Naming Conventions Exist for APTs

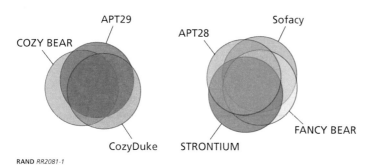

RAND RR2081-1

## Government Attribution Claims Are Often Political and Opaque

Governments may view cyber attacks conducted against its citizens, organizations, and industries as attacks to which it must respond. As such, the victim government may undertake an investigation and make a unilateral claim of attribution by publicly identifying the alleged attacker in an effort to 'name and shame' them and to prepare for follow-on network-defense and cost-imposition activities. However, these public claims of attribution have not been regularly issued or done in a consistent manner. In the multitude of cyber attacks, governments have publicly attributed the source in only a very few number of cases. Despite claiming to be regularly victimized by cyber attacks, Chinese officials have even suggested that attribution is nearly impossible (Sulmeyer and Chang, 2017; Segal, 2017). In the rare cases where governments have issued public attribution, the statements are issued at various levels of government, with various levels of formality, and are done through a variety of means. Often, the government refuses to share the information that led to its conclusions in order to protect sensitive sources and methods. In other cases, government officials speculate broadly about the source of an attack, sometimes even before an investigation has been conducted.

Following the Sony Pictures attack and the intrusions into the DNC, the U.S. government issued public attribution through statements by cabinet officials or the President. Whether these statements were considered persuasive depended in part on one's perception of the credibility of those officials. Additional, more-technical analysis reports were also released. However, these statements included little evidentiary information and were subject to public scrutiny and requests for the evidential basis.[10] They also came months after the initial incident and long after other cybersecurity researchers had already publicly offered

---

[10] A variety of experts —e.g., Lee (2016) and Deibert (2017)—have raised issues with the *GRIZZLY STEPPE* report. Regarding security researchers' doubts about Sony, see Rogers (2014).

their views. In other cases, the U.S. government has publicly attributed cyber incidents to state actors in the Chinese, Iranian, and Russian governments via law enforcement indictments, but these also provided little evidentiary basis for the findings (U.S. Department of Justice, 2014; 2016; 2017). Since these indicted actors would not likely be extradited and apprehended by U.S. law enforcement, the indictments led to questions about their overall point and effectiveness. In the case of the OPM attack, the U.S. government still has not made a public claim of attribution despite a widespread perception that Chinese state actors were responsible.

The United States is not unique in publicizing attribution without disclosing evidence. In other countries, attribution claims are regularly made without clear evidential support. For example, the Security Service of Ukraine publicly blamed the Russian government for the cyber attack on its power grid in 2015, even before the Ukrainian energy ministry had set up a special commission to investigate (Polityuk, 2015). Various elements of the Bangladesh government accused a range of actors for conducting the attack on the Central Bank. Public attribution from government officials without comprehensive evidence muddles the attribution claim and can pose a challenge to credibility.

This type of challenge to credibility, however, is not strictly limited to governments. There have been reports that some major private cybersecurity firms have affiliations with government agencies. Kaspersky Lab, for example, has been accused of turning a blind eye toward suspected Russian attacks (Matlack, Riley, and Robertson, 2015; Shachtman, 2012). Similarly, FireEye was financed in part by In-Q-Tel, the CIA's investment fund, and its CEO has expressed reservations about publicizing U.S.-backed attacks (Yadron, 2015). Having only one firm investigate an attack with geopolitical ramifications leaves a publicized attribution open to questions of partisanship.

Some commentators have suggested that governments should publicize attribution findings more regularly and rapidly as a routine matter of policy. Although this might regularize attribution claims and make them seemingly less ad hoc, many, if not most, governments lack the basic technical expertise, intelligence capability, and other resources to conduct their own investigations. Furthermore, governments have been reluctant to make public pronouncements because once they have identified the responsible party, they will face pressure to produce an effective and public response—a challenge for even the most capable states.

These issues suggest that governments may not be the most credible spokespersons for attribution findings. This challenge is sharpened in the current climate of public mistrust in political institutions.

## Collaboration Within the Private Sector Is Helpful

Cyber victims frequently rely on private-sector firms to conduct investigations. When private-sector cybersecurity firms work alone to attribute an attack on behalf of a victim, there is the risk that financial incentives motivate them to make attribution judgments quickly and beyond the evidentiary basis. Firms operating independently also do not undertake independent review and might be subject to influence by government authorities (Lin, 2016). Collaboration among a broad set of private-sector cybersecurity firms may overcome these challenges by providing outside review and additional quality control. Numerous examples of informal and formal collaboration among competing firms exist, and this collaboration and information-sharing has helped promote broader cybersecurity. Piggybacking analysis and formal collaboration can take advantage of core competencies spread across the various researchers and create a platform for rigorous examination of evidence.

Cases of informal collaboration among firms in cybersecurity include adoption of standardized methods and sharing of malware signatures and hashes. For instance, the Common Vulnerability Exposure (CVE) dictionary has grown from 29 members in 2000 to more than 150 today.[11] Similarly, the YARA tool is used by dozens of major cybersecurity firms, such as CrowdStrike, Symantec, and Kaspersky Lab (YARA, undated).

Cases of formal collaboration or piggyback collaboration on cyber attribution can lead to a streamlining of tasks based on core competencies and a final result based on multilateral analysis. Stuxnet, for example, was discovered by one relatively small security firm, but snowballed into a global effort spread among multiple companies with different core competencies: Microsoft issued operating system patches; antivirus companies like Symantec analyzed code and deployed malware signatures; and other security firms published useful post-mortems online. Operation Blockbuster (see Case Study 5, p. 42) serves as a separate model, not only of how private firms can agree to work together to build a body of knowledge on a major cyber threat, but also of how a collaborative approach can support state-level attribution, even when it was not the effort's intended goal (Novetta Threat Research Group, 2016).

## Transitioning from Insight to Action

These insights about attribution practice suggest a messy picture with respect to the current practice of public attribution. A variety of actors have sought to announce attribution statements, but there are lingering doubts about their technical competence, integrity, and objectivity.

---

[11] According to the CVE website, 29 organizations participated in the declarations of compatibility in December 2000. In 2017, there are more than 150 organizations listed on the CVE website (CVE, 2017).

The lack of consistent attribution methodology and standards makes it challenging to assess the merits of attribution claims. In the past, government public attribution claims were tailored toward narrow purposes, and are based on limited publicly released information. This unorganized environment enables malicious actors to hide their tracks more easily among myriad inconsistent judgments. These key insights suggest the importance of a collaborative and standardized approach to attribution investigations and public pronouncements, as the next chapter will demonstrate. Chapter Five will build on these insights to explore the core features of an independent organization for cyber attribution.

# CHAPTER FOUR

# Toward a Global Consortium for Cyber Attribution

The preceding discussion has described a fragmented landscape of cyber attribution that includes a range of actors working from an array of frameworks and that publicize findings in diffuse ways. While these actors have largely worked independently, they have also collaborated in specific cases. In addition to actual examples of collaboration, there have been proposals for new types of formalized mechanisms—in particular, Microsoft and authors of an Atlantic Council paper have both proposed the creation of an attribution body modeled after the IAEA (Smith, 2017; Healey et al., 2014).[1]

Figure 2 displays a set of alternative approaches to collaborative attribution investigations and how these attribution approaches were applied to cyber incidents in the past or could be applied to cyber incidents in the future. In the figure, the vertical axis is organized into three categories representing the participation of entities in an attribution investigation: state (government) entities, nonstate entities, or both state and nonstate entities. The horizontal axis is used to indicate the degree of sustained, formal collaboration between two or more entities engaged in an attribution investigation. The figure also includes a sample of cyber incident investigations indicating the incident name followed by the investigating entities in parentheses. For investigating entities that do not yet exist (those being proposed) or investigating entities that have not been applied to an incident covered in this report, we only show the entities in parentheses without a corresponding incident name. For example, we list the APT1 threat as involving very little sustained, formal collaboration because Mandiant (later acquired by FireEye), as a private firm, engaged in its own analysis and produced the nomenclature with limited formal

**There have been several proposals for the creation of a cyber attribution body, including one modeled after the IAEA.**

---

[1] In a 2014 Atlantic Council paper, several writers proposed the creation of a multilateral cyber adjudication and attribution council that would "provide an international mechanism for arriving at a consensus attribution of illegal cyber campaigns by states and a formal process for adjudicating associated interstate disputes" (Healey et al., 2014). The Microsoft proposal has also been discussed in Charney et al. (2016). A 2016 RAND report also discussed options and challenges regarding formal attribution mechanisms—see Harold et al. (2016).

FIGURE 2
Options for Collaborative Attribution Investigations

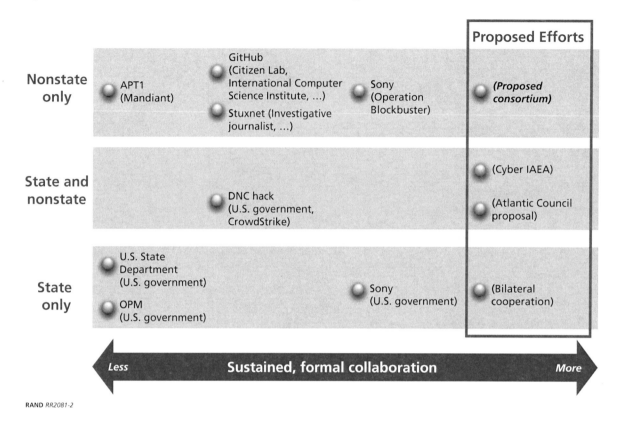

RAND RR2081-2

collaboration (see Case Study 3, p. 28). The Stuxnet virus largely involved analysis by researchers at Symantec but because it leveraged the discovery from non-Symantec employee Sergey Ulasen, as well as ad-hoc input from industrial controls companies, we shifted its position slightly to the right of that for APT1. While these various private firms investigated how Stuxnet was executed, an attribution of the attack to Israel and the United States was declared by, among other sources, a *New York Times* investigative journalist, David Sanger (2012), whose work may have been partly based on (possibly unofficially permitted) leaks. As another example, the Operation Blockbuster organization engaged in a collaborative investigation of the Sony Pictures hack but the collaboration has yet to be applied to another incident publicly.

Our analysis suggests the importance of a collaborative approach to attribution. It also suggests the value of a formalized model to facilitate a campaign approach and the value of a standing body to select cases for investigation through a normalized and transparent process. Lastly, our analysis suggests that, although states offer unique intelligence capabilities for attribution, their involvement can create complications that have a negative impact on the objectivity, transparency, and independence of the finding. Hence, our proposed model is shown in the top right of Figure 2, indicating nonstate participation in a sustained, formalized collaboration.

Figure 2 does not identify all the modes that state and nonstate actors have employed to work to attribute cyber attacks. For instance, the international police organization INTERPOL has undertaken a variety of initiatives to facilitate international cooperation to combat cyber crime, including sharing best practices that help law enforcement overcome attribution challenges (INTERPOL, 2016). It is also worth noting the Budapest Convention on Cybercrime and its role in cyber crime investigations involving multiple nations. This treaty, adopted by 56 states (as of December 2016), harmonizes domestic cyber crime laws and facilitates sharing of digital evidence across borders (Council of Europe, Treaty Office, 2001). One key challenge with international cyber investigations is that many states still lack the substantive and procedural legal frameworks and the forensic capabilities to acquire digital evidence. Increased international cooperation on cyber crime, such as that enabled by the Budapest Convention and INTERPOL, might assist in providing evidence for attribution investigations. However, our proposed consortium would not be dependent on state agreement to the Budapest Convention, nor would it have the narrow focus on law enforcement responses to cyber crime associated with INTERPOL.

## Mission

In light of the challenges and insights discussed here, we propose and explore the nature of an international organization for cyber attribution, which, for purposes of this analysis, we have named the Global Cyber Attribution Consortium (the Consortium). The mission of the organization is for a broad team of international experts to conduct independent investigations of major cyber incidents for the purpose of attribution. The Consortium would work with victims or their advocates upon request and with their cooperation to investigate cyber incidents using a diverse set of methodologies and would publish its findings for public review. The international community could use the Consortium's findings to bolster network defenses, thwart future attacks, and pursue follow-on enforcement actions to hold the perpetrator(s) accountable. In addition to providing a credible and transparent judgment of attribution, the Consortium's investigations would help standardize diffuse methodological approaches, naming conventions, and confidence metrics that would advance shared understanding in cyberspace and promote global cybersecurity.

## Membership and Legitimacy

It is crucial that the Consortium includes broad membership across geopolitical lines to foster a diversity of perspectives and to minimize the possibility that its findings are tainted by political influence. Based

# Mandiant Attribution of APT1 to Chinese Government

In February 2013, the private cyber security firm Mandiant (later acquired by FireEye) published a report linking the theft of hundreds of terabytes of data from at least 141 victims (of which 115 were located in the United States) in 20 major industries over a span of seven years to four large networks in China. They named the group involved in the attacks "APT1" (also known as "Comment Crew" by other firms) and described it as "one of the most prolific cyber espionage groups in terms of the sheer quantity of information stolen." Mandiant further concluded on the totality of their evidence that APT1 was government-employed, or at least known to the Chinese government, and suggested that APT1 was the 2nd Bureau of the People's Liberation Army General Staff Department's 3rd Department, also known as Unit 61398 (Mandiant, 2013).

In support of their conclusions, Mandiant described the physical locations of the buildings they believed housed the facilities used in the attacks they researched, and revealed three people they believed were associated with APT1. They also released more than 3,000 indicators of compromise (IOCs) to "bolster defenses against APT1 operations." The IOCs that Mandiant released included domain names, IP addresses, MD5 hashes of malware from more than 40 families, and 13 X.509 encryption certificates.

Mandiant itself acknowledged that there were downsides to publishing their conclusions and IOCs. Specifically, they acknowledged that publishing IOCs shortens their lifespan and therefore would make defenders' jobs more difficult. Mandiant reasoned, however, that establishing a connection to China would shed light on the ongoing threat originating there (as perceived by Mandiant) and lead to coordination in countering such threats.

The report was not without controversy. In a press briefing, China's Foreign Ministry spokesman characterized Mandiant's claim as "groundless criticism" and said it was "irresponsible and unprofessional" ("China Opposes Hacking Allegation: FM Spokesman," 2013). A spokesman for the Chinese Ministry of Defense also refuted Mandiant's conclusions, claiming the report lacked technical proof and that IP addresses can be stolen ("Chinese Military Never Supports Cyberattacks: Defense Ministry," 2013; Blanchard, 2013). Separately, executives at other firms criticized the report. Jeffrey Carr, CEO of Taia Global, for example, published a blog post (2013) in which he pointed out "critical analytic flaws" in Mandiant's report. Carr claimed Mandiant did not satisfactorily rule out other actors or false flags.

on analysis of cyber attribution cases and noncyber investigatory organizations and processes, our recommendation is that membership includes representatives from two sectors: (1) technical experts from cybersecurity and information technology companies, as well as academia, and (2) cyberspace policy experts, legal scholars, and international policy experts from a diversity of academia and research organizations.[2] There are existing examples of these actors sharing information and collaborating to achieve Internet governance and cybersecurity goals.[3] We envision membership of the Consortium to be between 20 and 40 expert representatives drawn from organizations within these sectors and for investigations to be conducted by small teams—often fewer than 10 investigators—who would have primary responsibility for reviewing technical forensics. Based on skill sets, different members may have different roles within an investigation, including technical assessment—as well as investigation versus judgment roles. The remaining representatives would provide oversight of the investigation, Red Team the initial findings, and provide input and feedback as appropriate.

Importantly, our recommendation is that state representatives not be operating members of the Consortium. States are not necessary for attribution in all cases because the private sector and technical community already possess significant expertise to attribute to various degrees in key cases without leveraging states and their unique intelligence capabilities—for instance, in the cases of APT1, Sony, and the DNC. There are also many smaller-scale attacks where independent researchers have attributed without state assistance.[4] Despite the capabilities of some states to conduct forensic investigations and to integrate unique all-source intelligence, our analysis underscores three reasons why states should not be officially represented:

1. States' attribution claims are often based on evidence and intelligence that they are not willing to publicly share, which engender persistent questions about how their findings were reached and whether they are credible.
2. States make public attribution claims for political purposes, and, as members, they would have reason to shape the Consortium's findings to serve their national interests.

---

[2] Examples of possible organizations might include: Kaspersky, Symantec, Crowd-Strike, Microsoft, Huawei, ZTE, the Internet Engineering Task Force (IETF), the Institute of Electrical and Electronics Engineers, the Internet Society, and the Tallinn Manual International Group of Experts.

[3] For instance, consider the variety of collaboration in Internet governance bodies such as the ICANN, IETF, and the information-sharing efforts to promote cybersecurity in Information Sharing and Analysis Centers.

[4] For example, see Brian Krebs' blog, *Krebs on Security*, with respect to instances of cyber crime.

3. States would have incentives to influence what cyber incidents the Consortium would investigate, and they would seek to steer the Consortium away from accepting cases that might shed light on or otherwise threaten their own cyber operations.

For these reasons, we believe that the credibility and transparency of the Consortium requires that it operate without standing state participation. Supportive states might play a helpful role by volunteering information to the Consortium to assist in an investigation, and the Consortium itself can decide whether to solicit this information and whether it should factor into an investigation. However, official membership should be restricted to a select set of nonstate parties carefully chosen to ensure global representativeness and technical competency. This restriction of membership also will enable the Consortium to coalesce as a body without depending on major cyber powers reaching agreement on the desirability and structure of the organization—a negotiation that could drag on for many years and might never be reached. We recognize that some private companies and organizations have affiliations with national governments, but we posit that a sufficient diversity of technical expertise, and the investigation procedures and governance mechanisms further described below, should mitigate concerns that state-proxy representatives will be able to interfere or alter attribution findings.

Given the limited consensus between states on cyberspace norms and the likelihood that a formal cybersecurity treaty is not possible in the short term, the Consortium would not derive its authority from existing or new international agreements. Rather, its legitimacy will be based on its reputation and credibility gained from the technical expertise of its diverse global membership and its commitment to objectivity and transparency in its attribution findings. The Consortium will build its reputation and credibility over time by publicly conducting attribution investigations and adhering to the publishing and review protocols discussed further below.

We acknowledge that there will be certain cyber attacks for which government intelligence is necessary to make an attribution decision. In cases where the Consortium determines that it is not equipped to confidently arrive at an attribution decision, the Consortium can make a declaration that government intelligence is needed. This process of private-sector firms indicating an inability to perform an attribution investigation has happened in the past.[5] More broadly, the Consortium will associate a confidence level with any attribution decision it makes, and the confidence level might be derived from the (un)availability of intelligence or such factors as the presence of false flags. (See

---

[5] For instance, in the Operation Blockbuster report, Novetta stopped short of state attribution but stated their work could bolster the attribution work of others (Novetta Threat Research Group, 2016).

"Attribution Confidence Standards" in Chapter Five for more discussion on confidence levels.)

## Analogous International Organizations

To inform the proposed organizational structure and subsequent functions of the Consortium, we reviewed a select group of international organizations that have loosely similar remits. Table 2 provides examples of analogous international organizations. The following international organizations, multistakeholder organizations, one-off investigatory processes, and national bodies are examples that provide insight on Consortium organization and functions. None of these organizations provide a perfect model for the Consortium, but they do offer lessons on its possible structure.

*Intergovernmental organizations*, such as those associated with the United Nations (including the IAEA and the International Telecommunications Union [ITU]), have recognized authority derived from formal state agreements and include broad state participation and technical expertise. They have various degrees of effectiveness at tackling specific international challenges and coordinating action among the global community, including, in the case of the IAEA, with technical verification and compliance. However, as previously explained, there are compelling reasons why state parties should be excluded from operational membership in the Consortium. Further, the Consortium's agility, technical competency, and ability to reach rough-consensus findings would be severely hampered if modeled after international bodies that include the entire global community and that are regularly characterized by unwieldy management and organizational overreach.

The UN Terrorist Sanctions Committee, whose membership includes the UN Security Council, provides a helpful example of a much smaller body that collaborates to assess technical evidence and reach consensus conclusions that are then published widely. However, that body is focused on nonstate terrorist threats, thereby enabling state representatives to more readily grapple with a shared problem. The Consortium, on the other hand, would need to be open to attributing cyber attacks

TABLE 2

## Analogous International Organizations

| INTERGOVERNMENTAL ORGANIZATIONS | INTERNATIONAL INVESTIGATIONS | MULTISTAKEHOLDER BODIES |
|---|---|---|
| IAEA | 2010 *Cheonan* sinking investigation | IETF |
| UN 1267 Terrorist Sanctions Committee | 2014 downing of Malaysia Airlines Flight 17 | Operation Blockbuster |
| OPCW | 2014–2016 Ebola investigation | ICANN |
| ITU | — | SWIFT |

to state actors, and would require technical proficiency from a range of actors not represented in the UN Security Council.

The OPCW provides a compelling example of a non-UN-based independent intergovernmental organization that leverages technical expertise to decrease the risks associated with the use of chemical weapons. Like the IAEA and the ITU, however, the OPCW is based on state affirmation of a formal treaty. Although some have proposed a similar type of arms control or ban for cyber capabilities, the U.S. government (among others) has explicitly stated it would not support the development of such an instrument. As a result, the Consortium cannot leverage a standing international agreement to derive its authority and functions.

*International investigations* provide some helpful lessons for how a diverse set of actors can collaborate to attribute international wrong-doing to responsible parties, including to states. Investigations such as the multinational investigation into the 2010 sinking of the Republic of Korea's *Cheonan* warship demonstrates the value of publicly revealing the technical evidence that supported an attribution finding to a state. The Dutch-led investigation into the downing of Malaysia Airlines Flight 17 also shared compelling technical analysis that pointed to Russian units operating in Eastern Ukraine. The Dutch team's findings were reinforced and made more precise through open-source research conducted by the nongovernment organization Bellingcat, demonstrating the potential role for outsiders to play in reviewing and bolstering official findings (Bellingcat, 2016). Although the findings in the *Cheonan* and Malaysia Airlines cases were denied by North Korea and Russia, respectively, the international nature of the investigation and publication of compelling technical details have produced general consensus of the credibility of the findings.

Despite these valuable lessons, the Consortium should not be directly modeled on these investigations because in all these cases, operational collaboration ceased once the case was resolved. As we have previously argued, cyber attribution requires a "campaign" rather than a one-off approach. The Consortium must have the capacity and capability to assess a multitude of potentially linked attacks, rather than take them individually. Further, a standing body can select the cases that it will investigate through a regularized and transparent process.

*Multistakeholder bodies* include representation from the private sector and civil society—not just states—and in this way they provide a useful membership model for the Consortium. Some of these bodies also demonstrate that a diversity of technical experts can successfully cooperate on Internet and cybersecurity issues. However, Internet governance organizations such as ICANN and the IETF have a diffuse open membership policy and a variety of technical objectives, whereas the Consortium should have an established and small group of members and be narrowly focused on its attribution mission. The Novetta-led Operation Blockbuster included a coalition of technology industry partners providing independent assessment that underscored the U.S. government's attribution finding, but was limited to a single cyber incident (see Case Study 5, p. 42). Project Grey Goose, founded in 2008 by Jeffrey Carr, was another organization that engaged in cyber attribution investigations (Carr, 2012). The investigations were based on crowd-sourced participation by a group of vetted, expert volunteers (Sterling, 2009). The first investigation by Project Grey Goose considered cyber attacks during the Russo-Georgian War.

## Differences Between Other Proposals for a Global Organization

Our analysis is not the first to consider the value of an international cyber attribution organization. Most notably, Microsoft and the Atlantic Council advocate increased global coordination on the issue of cyber attribution—and, indeed, Microsoft sponsored our research. All three discussions agree that there is value in an international attribution organization (Charney et al., 2016; Healey et al., 2014). However, our analysis arrives at two different conclusions concerning the design and function of the organization. First, unlike Microsoft and the Atlantic Council, and for reasons expressed earlier in this report, our research suggests that the attribution organization should be managed and operated independently from states. Second, the proposal in the Atlantic Council paper also contemplates an enforcement role for the organization. Our analysis leads us to oppose this function. Further discussion on the core functions of our proposal can be found in the next chapter.

# The Multifaceted Attribution Process of the DNC Attack

Starting in 2015, the DNC suffered a cyber intrusion amid a contentious presidential election. The intruders exfiltrated files and emails, many of which were publicly released by WikiLeaks, causing confusion within the DNC and the resignation of its chair, Debbie Wasserman Schultz. While it is difficult, if not impossible, to estimate the full damage of the attack, it is widely considered to have played a role in the 2016 U.S. presidential election.

Investigation of the attack was led by the private cybersecurity firm CrowdStrike, which publicly assessed in May and June 2016 that two Russian APTs were responsible: FANCY BEAR (associated with the Russian GRU) and COZY BEAR (associated with the Russian FSB) (Alperovitch, 2016). As evidence, CrowdStrike referenced, in part, the use of exploits via Powershell, C2 infrastructure via AdobeARM, and the use of previously witnessed timestamps and strings. For example, some of the DNC malware included a self-delete function called "seppuku" (Buratowski, 2016). This identically named function was also found in code used in other attacks starting in 2010, according to Symantec (Symantec Security Response, 2015). CrowdStrike shared its data with other privacy cyber services firms, as well as several U.S. intelligence agencies.

The U.S. government performed a follow-up investigation. On October 7, before the election, the Department of Homeland Security and DNI released an unprecedented joint statement attributing the incident to "senior most officials" of the Russian government. However, the statement did not provide any evidence for the finding (U.S. Department of Homeland Security and DNI, 2016). In the midst of public clamor for more information, the Department of Homeland Security and the FBI released a Joint Analysis Report titled *GRIZZLY STEPPE* that identified technical details and tools used by the Russian actors (U.S. Department of Homeland Security and FBI, 2016). This report was also widely criticized by the technical community and provided limited additional evidence of attribution. Following the election, and in the final days of the Obama administration, DNI released a coordinated intelligence report providing additional details on the Russia campaign (DNI, 2017). However, like other U.S. government statements, the analysis did not publicly provide significant additional evidence of attribution, with the explanation that sources and methods needed to be protected.

WikiLeaks did not reveal the source of its information, but shortly after the initial attributions, the attack was claimed by an unknown actor known as "Guccifer 2.0." Investigations found that the Guccifer 2.0 moniker was likely a ruse used to cover the tracks of Russian state actors; for example, the claim included the release of a Microsoft Word document with metadata indicating that the document was of Russian origin (Goodin, 2016). Russia dissented over the attribution claims.

# CHAPTER FIVE

# The Core Features of a Cyber Attribution Organization

Our analysis of existing bodies and processes reveals that the Global Cyber Attribution Consortium's investigatory process and findings should include the following six core features:

- Formal Triggering Condition Standards
- Evidence-Collection Process
- Evidence-Assessment Framework
- Attribution Confidence Standards
- Notification and Public Statement Procedures
- Severity and Sophistication Assessment Procedures.

Across all of these core features, the Consortium should be guided by the following principles: It should have technical competency, impartiality, inclusivity, and a narrow focus. It should also be consensus-driven.

## Formal Triggering Condition Standards

One of the core features of the Consortium is its ability to be selective about what cases to take from the population of cyber incidents. In a world where cyber attacks can range from relatively pedestrian DDoS or ransomware attacks to attacks that impair nuclear reactors and threaten power grids, the range of available cases to investigate is enormous. In light of this, an attribution organization like the Consortium needs the ability to pick and choose instances worthy of review.

In this way, the Consortium is designed as an organization that has a discretionary docket—that is, it alone determines which cases to take on for investigation from among those submitted for review. We propose a basic process similar to that of the U.S. Supreme Court. Out of approximately 7,000–8,000 petitions submitted to the Court every year, the justices choose about 80 cases to hear (U.S. Supreme Court, undated). Two elements of this process are worthy of note. First, the request for review is initiated by an aggrieved party. For cyber attribution, this is the

The Consortium should have technical competency, impartiality, inclusivity, and a narrow focus. It should also be consensus-driven.

victim of the attack. Granting the victim the exclusive right of initiation preserves the victim's privacy, autonomy, and ability to determine whether and when to seek an attribution investigation.[1] There are open questions about who precisely might constitute the "victim" of a cyber attack—for instance, was the victim of the Ukraine electrical grid attack the electrical control center, the Ukrainian government, the consumers who lost power, or the hardware and software developers whose vulnerabilities were exploited? We propose that the Consortium can use its own discretion about who constitutes a victim and thus is positioned to bring a case forward. Second, mere application for review is not sufficient to trigger action. Just because a victim requests the Consortium's assistance should not mean that the Consortium will take the case.

The discretionary nature of the Consortium's portfolio of cases provides opportunities to establish two essential matters of self-determination: the criteria that should be used to assess whether a victim's petition for review of a cyber attack (either a single instance or a prolonged series or campaign of attacks) is significant enough to merit review; and the decision rule by which the principals who run the Consortium should decide whether to take a case. Regarding the criteria the Consortium might use, there are both internal and case-specific constraints to consider. Case-specific constraints concern the nature of the alleged attack: how many people or systems were compromised, what level of economic or reputational harm was caused, etc. Internal constraints are institutional concerns: availability of financial resources to the Consortium, time, technical capabilities, etc. These will limit the Consortium's ability to hear cases, regardless of the interest, importance, or severity of the petitions.

Beyond these case-specific and institutional constraints, however, the Consortium must also think about the decision rule: What is the process by which Consortium administrators decide to take a case? Here, again, the analogy to the U.S. Supreme Court is instructive. In order for the Court to hear a case, a minority of justices (four out of nine) is the minimum vote required to hear the case. This is an instance of a minority setting the agenda, even though a majority decides the ultimate issue. For the Consortium, a decision rule that grants the minority the right to set the docket could allow for a greater diversity of types of cases to come up for review.

## Evidence-Collection Process

To enable the determination of attribution, the Consortium will need to have access to all relevant data, much of which will reside on the victim's computer network (e.g., log files and browser histories discussed

---

[2] Victims are also essential in granting access to internal data and networks that hold clues as to the identity of the cyber attackers. Without a victim willing to provide access to compromised networks, the attribution efforts are likely to be inconclusive.

earlier). It is our belief that the victim's request for an investigation will imply a willingness on the part of the victim to make computer networking data and assets available to the Consortium. This willingness to cooperate is in stark contrast to many intergovernmental investigation processes. In some cases, there is in adversarial relationship between the investigatory institution and the nation whose activity must be investigated. For example, the challenge of addressing nuclear proliferation often places the IAEA in a policing role.

Even though the relationship between the Consortium and the victim may be cooperative, there are still risks to be considered and the evidence-collection process must be properly defined. The Consortium will need to specify the data to be collected from both the victim and elsewhere, including details about the kinds of artifacts to be reviewed, the process by which these artifacts will be accessed, and the duration for which access will be granted. The kind of data specified by the evidence-collection process will depend on the current practices of cyber attacks and attribution investigations; hence, these data specifications will likely evolve over time and it will likely be the case that the Consortium will play a role in capturing this evolution in its published evidence-collection procedure.

It is likely that the evidence associated with a given investigation will involve sensitive data that might include intellectual property related to the victim. For this reason, confidentiality agreements will be entrusted to help protect any information discovered during the investigation that is not directly related to the cyber breach.

Other third parties—including network operators, security researchers, or even states—might also have evidence to contribute to the investigation, and the Consortium will need a process to collect and protect relevant voluntarily shared information from these sources.

## Evidence-Assessment Framework

In moving forward with an international organization responsible for facilitating cyber attribution, the organization should clearly define and publish the analytic framework upon which evidence shall be assessed. As comparing incidents and methods can be useful in supporting attribution across a campaign of attacks, a mechanism for attack comparison is also likely to be included in the evidence-assessment framework.

Analysis should involve some degree of weighting of individual pieces of evidence; for example, technical indicators may be weighted more heavily than nontechnical indicators, and those technical indicators that are more prone to deception may be weighted less heavily than other technical indicators. Weighting the evidence can help in establishing levels of confidence in claims of attribution.

The assessment process should involve deploying Consortium members independently to analyze evidence. This helps address concerns that private firms may have about exposing intellectual property and/or proprietary methods that they believe may give them a competitive advantage. Once the independent research is complete, the Consortium would seek a consensus conclusion based on the individual findings of the Consortium members. If the Consortium fails to reach a unanimous decision, majority and minority opinions shall be recorded in a manner similar to U.S. Supreme Court decisions. As in the Court, minority opinions may hold future value for the Consortium. Additionally, the Consortium may allow for members to reserve comment or recuse themselves altogether, if doing so is beneficial to the member and/or the Consortium.

## Attribution Confidence Standards

The ultimate product of the Consortium effort is an attribution of responsibility for an incident or attack. Following the Consortium's work using the evidence-assessment framework and multiple methodologies contributed by Consortium members, the organization will need to devise processes for communicating two essential pieces of information: who the Consortium believes is responsible based on the evidence and methodologies used by the investigators, and how confident they are in that assessment. Both pieces of information are crucial for the validity and reputation of the Consortium as an independent attribution organization.

The efforts toward identifying who is responsible for an incident or attack will be influenced and potentially hindered by the available evidence and methodologies used by the investigators. As discussed earlier, identifying specific individuals as responsible for an incident or attack is likely to be challenging—in some cases, it will be impossible. Furthermore, attributing an attack as fully commanded and controlled by state entities (as opposed to individuals within geographic territories) will be even more difficult, although in some cases such evidence may be discoverable.

These limitations on the Consortium's ability to pinpoint specific individuals, or allege state-sponsorship through formal C2 structures, as responsible for incidents or attacks highlight the need for the Consortium to be clear in what evidence they have and how strong the evidence is behind their conclusions. Hence, the Consortium should establish and rigorously adhere to a set of analytic standards that details how the Consortium will produce and evaluate its analyses. Sample analytic standards are available from DNI, which faces similar challenges in communicating the confidence of information that underlies their analytic conclusions (DNI, 2015). At its core, these standards are designed to ensure integrity; highlight the split between assumptions, judgments, and fact-based analysis; and highlight for the ultimate consumers of the analysis any areas of weak or missing evidence so as to mitigate future errors in judgment.

The Consortium will be judged on the quality of its investigations and assessments. Adhering to best-in-practice analytic standards will help the Consortium to earn a reputation as a trusted source in cyber attack attribution.

## Notification and Public Statement Procedures

The organization will inform relevant parties of its key findings prior to issuing a public statement or releasing a public report outlining its assessment. Before the organization issues a public statement, there will be a well-defined period during which relevant parties may offer responses or critiques of the findings. This process may include the submission of additional information or alternative assessments.

We believe it is important that the Consortium reports all findings to the public. Given the complexity and secrecy of cyber operations, informing the public about the identity and methods used to commit cyber attacks may help bolster the attribution finding and enable further accountability mechanisms. It will also help network defenders integrate the information into their defensive systems so that they can guard against the responsible actor, patch exploited vulnerabilities, identify TTP, and remedy compromised infrastructure.

In addition to openness and transparency, there are several other objectives the Consortium should pursue when providing information to the public. Public statements and reports should provide

- clear and timely information to the public about the Consortium's attribution actions and the rationale for those decisions
- transparency and evidence-based consensus (or majority/minority reports) in order to enhance legitimacy of the organization (Federal Open Market Committee, 2017)
- publishable technical details for broader assessment and discussion
- written and verbal statements that can be used as testimony in international and national deliberations or court hearings.

The Consortium should select from traditional forms of public communication, including written and verbal statements, decisions, minutes, reports, and transcripts (12 CFR 271, 2016). Communication should describe the investigatory actions and rationale for attribution decisions and might include

- synthesis of prior investigations
- description of technical evidence and their contribution to attribution
- confidence of attribution.

## Severity and Sophistication Assessment Procedures

The Consortium can also help reduce risk in cyberspace by assessing the severity of the cyber attack and its sophistication. A standardized process for severity assessment of cyber incidents will facilitate post-attribution actions. For example, a severity schema could be useful for institutions that choose to employ only new defensive measures in response to evidence that severe attacks have occurred against other entities. There are several ways in which severity could be measured. For instance, for attacks with physical damage (e.g., Stuxnet or the Ukrainian power grid attacks), the scale of physical costs may be used for severity assessment. Threats to the political independence of states (e.g., the DNC attacks) could also be used. Another severity assessment factor could be financial loss (e.g., the Sony Pictures attack). The Consortium could recommend standards for severity assessment that could be applied by others.

The severity assessment recommended by the Consortium may take inspiration from relevant models currently in practice. For example, a common definition used in major power grid failures is (1) an unplanned event (down for maintenance or rotating blackouts do not count) that (2) affects at least 1,000 customers (in this study, the number is 30,000 minimum) for (3) a total downtime of at least 1 million customer-hours (McLinn, 2009). The Federal Emergency Management Agency sets standards on the severity of major disasters. The U.S. government's own color-coded severity schema might provide a useful model (U.S. Department of Homeland Security, 2016).

The Consortium also might leverage its expertise and promote shared understanding in cyberspace by building a framework to assess the sophistication of a cyber attack. Commentators regularly use the concept of sophistication in an inconsistent manner and victims have incentives to exaggerate the sophistication of the threats they face. Although the sophistication of an attack does not necessarily correspond to impact—nor do advanced, well-resourced states only employ sophisticated techniques—a standardized assessment framework can help network defenders and the public better understand this complex terrain. There have been attempts to work out a sophistication framework, and the Consortium can explore and build off existing approaches.[2] Through regular use over time, the sophistication approach used by the Consortium might become standardized throughout the cybersecurity community.

## Enforcement and Legal Standards

It is important to reiterate our position that the Consortium should be narrowly focused on attribution and not subsequent action, such

---

[3] For one proposed framework, see Buchanan (2017).

as enforcement. The comparative advantage of the Consortium in this regard is that it will be composed of independent experts working to find a consensus attribution claim where possible with the support of evidence that can be released to the public. After an attribution claim has been made, the Consortium will not make recommendations for subsequent action (such as sentencing recommendations). Accordingly, it will make no punitive recommendations or referrals to other organizations (e.g., International Code Council, International Court of Justice, UN Security Council), as such referrals could be seen as tantamount to a recommendation for prosecution. At the same time, however, the victim, another nation, or an external organization may use the Consortium's attribution as the basis for taking further action as that party deems appropriate.

Furthermore, we principally see the role of the Consortium as providing a precise and accurate narrative and not providing evidence that would be used in a court of law (in the United States or other countries). Nevertheless, to the extent that evidence is found that violates existing or future international laws, such evidence would need to be made public in order to stand up against courtroom scrutiny. Opaque data from government intelligence would not suffice for such purposes unless it is declassified. Hence, the Consortium would be well positioned to provide cyber attack evidence meeting the legal standards of criminality if such evidence is found.

## Sony Pictures and Operation Blockbuster

The attack in November 2014 against Sony Pictures was a watershed moment for the public attribution of malicious cyber activity. The attack led to the release of sensitive information from the film studio, including personal information, corporate email, and unreleased Sony movies, and it significantly disrupted Sony Pictures business operations. A group calling itself the "Guardians of Peace" claimed responsibility for the attack, and threatened additional attacks—including physical attacks on movie theaters—if Sony continued its plan to release the film *The Interview*, a comedy depicting the assassination of the North Korean leader Kim Jong-Un.

In cooperation with Sony Pictures, the U.S. government conducted an investigation, culminating in a statement by the FBI concluding, "the North Korean government is responsible for these actions" (FBI, 2014). The FBI indicated three reasons they reached their conclusion. These reasons included:

> "[1] Technical analysis of the data deletion malware used in this attack revealed links to other malware that the FBI knows North Korean actors previously developed . . . [2] significant overlap between the infrastructure used in this attack and other malicious activity . . . linked to North Korea [and 3] the tools used in the [Sony] attack have similarities to a cyber attack . . . against South Korean banks . . . carried out by North Korea."

However, the statement noted that the FBI could not share the evidence used to make that assessment because of the "need to protect sensitive sources and methods."

Public perception of this attribution was mixed, with many noting that North Korea did have the means and motives to carry out the attack, while others found reasons to doubt the government's claims (e.g., Schneier, 2014). Many noted that the United States needed to be more explicit and transparent about its evidence (e.g., Zetter, 2014b).

In February 2016, the data and cyber analytics firm Novetta published Operation Blockbuster, a report summarizing a private-firm coalition effort to identify and disrupt the tools and tactics used by the Sony attackers (Novetta Threat Research Group, 2016). The coalition included a variety of cybersecurity firms, including Symantec, Kaspersky Labs, and Trend Micro, working in partnership to share and analyze cyber threat indicators associated with the attack. The report lays out its research methodology and presents a range of technical evidence connecting the Sony attack to the Lazarus Group. Although the report stops short of alleging North Korean state sponsorship, it provides a compelling example of how private firms can collaborate to reach an attribution finding and publicly present evidence.

# CHAPTER SIX

# Conclusion

I n the face of increasingly frequent cyber attacks and increasing severity of the effects of those attacks, interest in independent, reliable, and trusted attribution is paramount. Both public and private sectors are growing increasingly alarmed about the nature of cyber threats. To better prepare for, defend against, and investigate cyber events requires skilled professionals, knowledge-sharing, and organizations with the credibility and responsibility for identifying cyber attackers.

While ad hoc international efforts have been made to build widespread agreement on norms of behavior surrounding cyber activities—such as the push for agreement that critical infrastructure should be off-limits in nation-led cyber attacks—there are no extant systems for holding nations accountable. Furthermore, as the democratization of technology brings cyber capabilities to more and more individuals without the backing of states, the drive for accountability and compliance grows increasingly complicated.

At the core of all of these concerns, however, is the need to know who is responsible for cyber attacks when they occur. International norms and promises of good behavior are a step toward establishing expectations; however, without the ability to know when an attack has occurred and who is behind the effort, the greatest offenders are enabled to flout the international efforts. Thus, the ability to know who is responsible is the linchpin of accountability.

But the current state of play in cyber attribution is widely distributed and mired in competing interests of politics, business, and international affairs. States occasionally clash over attribution allegations. Private companies with cutting-edge methodologies for investigating cyber crimes regularly compete—but seldom coordinate—to advance verified information about the highest-profile cases of cyber attacks. And no one seems to have the final, trusted word in bringing about a consensus opinion on attribution.

This report has argued that the time may be right for a new international attribution organization. Drawing on lessons learned from a review of major cyber attacks of recent years, as well as from key insights from the state of the art of cyber attribution methods and tactics, we have offered a preliminary model of a new organization—the Global Cyber Attribution Consortium. Such an organization would be created

**The time may be right for a new international attribution organization.**

to provide independent investigation of major cyber incidents, by a broad team of international experts, for the purpose of attribution.

The unique strengths of the Consortium are its international composition; its ability to compile diverse methodologies, independently deployed by the constituent members of the Consortium; and its remit to produce a publicly announced consensus attribution (with opportunities for dissension) on the cases the Consortium decides to investigate. The Consortium would work with victims of cyber attacks on attribution matters; if warranted, victims, nations, and the international community could then devise strategies to bolster network defenses, thwart future attacks, and choose appropriate enforcement actions that would hold the responsible parties accountable. Given that our proposal cautions against state membership, a key weakness of the Consortium would be the lack of access to government intelligence resources that will be necessary for some attribution investigations.

This report sketches out some of the key attributes for an organization like the Consortium to consider, including:

- membership restricted to nongovernmental experts
- core features of its triggering conditions for taking a case
- an evidence-collection and evidence-assessment framework
- the need for attribution confidence standards
- public reporting requirements
- the development of attack severity and sophistication metrics.

These are just the beginning of the governance and operational dimensions that an organization like the Consortium must address. One important aspect of the Consortium that must be worked out prior to a successful launch includes funding. Given our assumption that membership will not consist of state representatives, the Consortium would face a funding challenge that many global organizations do not need to consider. Typically, multistate organizations, such as the United Nations and the North Atlantic Treaty Organization, are funded by fees charged to the member states. In this case, revenue from states would not likely be available or appropriate, even though states stand to receive a good deal of benefit from the Consortium's decisions. Furthermore, initial membership by private-sector firms is likely to be a challenge because the relative financial strength of these firms (and the associated ability to pay) spans a broad range and risks plutocratic optics.

One funding option is for philanthropic organizations to serve as a source of initial funding during the Consortium's infancy with a charter mandate to seek funding from a state-based organization, such as the United Nations, within a set period of time. While this approach risks the possibility of initial overinfluence by a philanthropic entity, it at least prepares a road map for the Consortium to transition to authority under an international organization with diverse and broad representation.

Another option is for telecommunications and information technology companies to fund the organization. Companies like Comcast, Verizon, Intel, or Microsoft provide the software and network hardware systems through which cyber attacks are carried out, as well as digital forensics tools for supporting analysis. They have a vested interest in, if not the obligation of, identifying and preventing the use of their networks to harm customers. Pooling resources across these companies may not only provide adequate funding but also may enhance the credibility and profile of the Consortium.

Further questions of staffing, administration, confidentiality, security, and even location of the organization are sure to raise deeper issues of organizational structure and function. While work remains on the establishment of any international attribution organization, the justification for such an organization is becoming increasingly apparent and the need increasingly dire.

# Abbreviations

| | |
|---|---|
| APT | Advanced Persistent Threat |
| C2 | command and control |
| CEO | chief executive officer |
| CIA | Central Intelligence Agency |
| DDoS | Distributed Denial of Service |
| DNA | deoxyribonucleic acid |
| DNC | Democratic National Committee |
| DNI | U.S. Office of the Director of National Intelligence |
| DNS | domain name system |
| FBI | Federal Bureau of Investigation |
| G20 | Group of 20 |
| IAEA | International Atomic Energy Agency |
| ICANN | Internet Corporation for Assigned Names and Numbers |
| IETF | Internet Engineering Task Force |
| IP | Internet Protocol |
| ISIS | Islamic State of Iraq and Syria |
| ITU | International Telecommunications Union |
| HUMINT | human intelligence |
| NASA | National Aeronautics and Space Administration |
| OPCW | Organization for the Prohibition of Chemical Weapons |
| OPM | Office of Personnel Management |
| OSINT | open-source intelligence |
| SIGINT | signals intelligence |
| SWIFT | Society for Worldwide Interbank Financial Telecommunication |
| TTP | tactics, techniques, and procedures |
| UN | United Nations |

# References

"AlienVault Ossim," web page, undated. As of May 26, 2017:
https://www.alienvault.com/products/ossim

Alperovitch, Dmitri, "Bears in the Midst: Intrusion into the Democratic National Committee," *CrowdStrike*, blog post, June 15, 2016. As of March 31, 2017:
https://www.crowdstrike.com/blog/
bears-midst-intrusion-democratic-national-committee/

AV Comparatives, *Data Transmission in Internet Security Products*, May 20, 2014. As of March 31, 2017:
http://www.av-comparatives.org/wp-content/uploads/2014/04/
avc_datasending_2014_en.pdf

Bartholomew, Brian, and Juan Andres Guerrero-Saade, *Wave Your False Flags! Deception Tactics Muddying Attribution in Targeted Attacks*, Virus Bulletin Conference, October 2016.

Baumgartner, Kurt, and Maria Garnaeva, "BE2 Custom Plugins, Router Abuse, and Target Profiles: New Observations on BlackEnergy2 APT Activity," *SecureList*, Kaspersky Lab website, November 3, 2014. As of March 31, 2017:
https://securelist.com/blog/research/67353/
be2-custom-plugins-router-abuse-and-target-profiles/

Bellingcat, "MH-17—The Open Source Investigation, Two Years Later," blog post, July 15, 2016. As of March 31, 2017:
https://www.bellingcat.com/news/uk-and-europe/2016/07/15/
mh17-the-open-source-investigation-two-years-later/

Blanchard, Ben, "China Says U.S. Hacking Accusations Lack Technical Proof," Reuters, Februry 20, 2013. As of March 31, 2017:
http://www.reuters.com/article/
us-china-hacking-idUSBRE91I06120130220

Buchanan, Ben, *The Legend of Sophistication In Cyber Operations*, Cambridge, Mass.: Belfer Center for Science and International Affairs, Harvard Kennedy School, January 2017. As of March 31, 2017:
https://www.belfercenter.org/sites/default/files/files/publication/
Legend%20Sophistication%20-%20web.pdf

Buratowski, Michael, "Findings from Analysis of DNC Intrusion Malware; Analyzing the DNC Malware," *Fidelis Cybersecurity*, blog post, June 20, 2016. As of March 31, 2017:
https://www.fidelissecurity.com/threatgeek/2016/06/
findings-analysis-dnc-intrusion-malware

Carr, Jeffrey, "Announcing Project Grey Goose—Operation Poachers," blog post, May 14, 2012. As of May 12, 2017: http://jeffreycarr.blogspot.com/2012/05/announcing-project-grey-goose-operation.html

———, "Mandiant APT1 Report Has Critical Analytic Flaws," blog post, February 19, 2013. As of March 31, 2017: http://jeffreycarr.blogspot.com/2013/02/mandiant-apt1-report-has-critical.html

Charney, Scott, Erin English, Aaron Kleiner, Nemanja Malisevic, Angela McKay, Jan Neutze, and Paul Nicholas, *From Articulation to Implementation: Enabling Progress on Cybersecurity Norms*, Microsoft Corporation, June 2016. As of March 31, 2017: https://mscorpmedia.azureedge.net/mscorpmedia/2016/06/Microsoft-Cybersecurity-Norms_vFinal.pdf

"China Opposes Hacking Allegation: FM Spokesman," *Xinhua*, February 19, 2013. As of March 31, 2017: http://news.xinhuanet.com/english/china/2013-02/19/c_132178666.htm

"Chinese Military Never Supports Cyberattacks: Defense Ministry," *Xinhua*, February 20, 2013. As of March 31, 2017: http://news.xinhuanet.com/english/china/2013-02/20/c_132180420.htm

Code of Federal Regulations, Title 12, Banks and Banking, Chapter II, Federal Reserve System (Continued), Subchapter B, Federal Open Market Committee, Part 271, Rules Regarding Availability of Information, January 1, 2016. As of March 31, 2017: https://www.gpo.gov/fdsys/search/pagedetails.action?sr=397&originalSearch=&st=his&ps=10&na=&se=&sb=re&timeFrame=&dateBrowse=&govAuthBrowse=&collection=&historical=false&packageId=CFR-2016-title12-vol4&fromState=&bread=true&granuleId=CFR-2016-title12-vol4-part271&collectionCode=CFR&browsePath=Title+12%2FChapter+II%2FSubchapter+B%2FPart+271

Common Vulnerabilities and Exposures, "About CVE," web page, February 23, 2017. As of March 31, 2017: https://cve.mitre.org/about/

Corera, Gordon, "How France's TV5 Was Almost Destroyed by 'Russian Hackers,'" BBC News, October 10, 2016. As of March 31, 2017: http://www.bbc.com/news/technology-37590375

Council of Europe, Treaty Office, "Convention on Cybercrime," Budapest, November 23, 2001. As of May 24, 2017: https://www.coe.int/en/web/conventions/full-list/-/conventions/treaty/185

CVE—*See* Common Vulnerabilities and Exposures.

DeCianno, Jessica, "Indicators of Attack vs. Indicators of Compromise," *CrowdStrike*, blog post, December 9, 2014. As of March 31, 2017:
https://www.crowdstrike.com/blog/
indicators-attack-vs-indicators-compromise/

Defense Science Board, *Resilient Military Systems and the Advanced Cyber Threat*, Washington, D.C.: U.S. Department of Defense, Task Force Report, January 2013. As of May 26, 2017:
http://www.dtic.mil/get-tr-doc/pdf?AD=ADA569975

Deibert, Ronald, "The DHS/FBI Report on Russian Hacking Was a Predictable Failure," *Just Security*, blog post, January 4, 2017. As of March 31, 2017:
https://www.justsecurity.org/35989/
dhsfbi-report-russian-hacking-predictable-failure/

DNI—*See* U.S. Office of the Director of National Intelligence.

Edwards, Benjamin, Alexander Furnas, Stephanie Forrest, and Robert Axelrod, "Strategic Aspects of Cyberattack, Attribution, and Blame," *Proceedings of the National Academy of Sciences of the United States of America*, Vol. 114, No. 11, March 14, 2017, pp. 2825–2830. As of March 31, 2017:
http://www.pnas.org/content/114/11/2825.abstract

Fagerland, Snorre, and Waylon Grange, *The Inception Framework: Cloud-Hosted APT*, Sunnyvale, Calif.: Blue Coat Systems, Inc., 2015. As of March 31, 2017:
https://www.bluecoat.com/documents/download/
638d602b-70f4-4644-aaad-b80e1426aad4/
d5c87163-e068-440f-b89e-e40b2f8d2088

Farrell, Paul, "History of 5-Eyes—Explainer," *The Guardian*, December 2, 2013. As of March 31, 2017:
https://www.theguardian.com/world/2013/dec/02/
history-of-5-eyes-explainer

FBI—*See* Federal Bureau of Investigation.

Federal Bureau of Investigation, "Update on Sony Investigation," press release, December 19, 2014. As of May 24, 2017:
https://www.fbi.gov/news/pressrel/press-releases/
update-on-sony-investigation

———, "A Primer on DarkNet Marketplaces," web page, November 1, 2016. As of March 31, 2017:
https://www.fbi.gov/news/
stories/a-primer-on-darknet-marketplaces

Federal Open Market Committee, "FOMC Policy on External Communications of Federal Reserve System Staff," Washington, D.C., January 31, 2017.

Finkle, Jim,"Cyber Security Firm: More Evidence North Korea Linked to Bangladesh Heist," Reuters, April 3, 2017. As of May 24, 2017:
http://www.reuters.com/article/
us-cyber-heist-bangladesh-northkorea-idUSKBN1752I4

G20, "G20 Leaders' Communiqué, Antalya Summit, 15–16 November 2015," 2015 Turkey G20 web page, undated. As of March 31, 2017:
http://g20.org.tr/g20-leaders-commenced-the-antalya-summit/

Goodin, Dan, "'Guccifer' Leak of DNC Trump Research Has a Russian's Fingerprints on It," *Ars Technica*, June 16, 2016. As of March 31, 2017:
https://arstechnica.com/security/2016/06/guccifer-leak-of-dnc-trump-research-has-a-russians-fingerprints-on-it/

GReAT, "BlackEnergy APT Attacks in Ukraine Employ Spearphishing with Word Documents," *SecureList*, Kaspersky Lab website, January 28, 2016. As of March 31, 2017:
https://securelist.com/blog/research/73440/
blackenergy-apt-attacks-in-ukraine-employ-
spearphishing-with-word-documents/

———, "Lazarus Under The Hood," *SecureList*, Kaspersky Lab website, April 3, 2017. As of March 31, 2017:
https://securelist.com/blog/sas/77908/lazarus-under-the-hood/

Groll, Elias, "'Obama's General' Pleads Guilty to Leaking Stuxnet Operation," *Foreign Policy*, October 17, 2016. As of May 24, 2017:
http://foreignpolicy.com/2016/10/17/
obamas-general-pleads-guilty-to-leaking-stuxnet-operation/

———, "NSA Official Suggests North Korea Was Culprit in Bangladesh Bank Heist," *Foreign Policy*, March 21, 2017. As of March 31, 2017:
http://foreignpolicy.com/2017/03/21/nsa-official-suggests-north-korea-was-culprit-in-bangladesh-bank-heist/

Harold, Scott Warren, Martin C. Libicki, and Astrid Cevallos, *Getting to Yes with China in Cyberspace*, Santa Monica, Calif.: RAND Corporation, RR-1335-RC, 2016. As of March 31, 2017:
http://www.rand.org/pubs/research_reports/RR1335.html

Healey, Jason, "Beyond Attribution: Seeking National Responsibility for Cyber Attacks," Atlantic Council Issue Brief, Washington, D.C., 2011. As of March 31, 2017:
http://www.atlanticcouncil.org/images/files/publication_pdfs/
403/022212_ACUS_NatlResponsibilityCyber.PDF

Healey, Jason, John C. Mallery, Klara Tothova Jordan, and Nathaniel V. Youd, *Confidence-Building Measures in Cyberspace: A Multistakeholder Approach for Stability and Security*, Washington, D.C.: Atlantic Council, November 2014. As of March 31, 2017:
http://www.atlanticcouncil.org/images/publications/
Confidence-Building_Measures_in_Cyberspace.pdf

Hilton, Scott, "Dyn Analysis Summary of Friday October 21 Attack," *Company News*, Dyn blog post, October 26, 2016. As of
March 31, 2017:
http://dyn.com/blog/
dyn-analysis-summary-of-friday-october-21-attack/

Hirschfeld Davis, Julie, "Hacking of Government Computers Exposed 21.5 Million People," *New York Times*, July 9, 2015. As of March 31, 2017:
https://www.nytimes.com/2015/07/10/us/
office-of-personnel-management-hackers-got-data-of-
millions.html

Industrial Control Systems Cyber Emergency Response Team, "Cyber-Attack Against Ukrainian Critical Infrastructure Alert (IR-ALERT-H-16-056-01)," US-CERT web page, February 25, 2016. As of March 31, 2017:
https://ics-cert.us-cert.gov/alerts/IR-ALERT-H-16-056-01

Internet Corporation for Assigned Names and Numbers, "About WHOIS," web page, undated. As of March 31, 2017:
https://whois.icann.org/en/about-whois

INTERPOL, "Identifying Cybercriminals at Core of INTERPOL-Europol Conference," web page, September 28, 2016. As of May 30, 2017:
https://www.interpol.int/News-and-media/News/2016/N2016-121

Kennedy, John, "The Five-Minute CIO: Alex Stamos, CSO, Facebook," *Silicon Republic*, November 11, 2016. As of May 26, 2017:
https://www.siliconrepublic.com/enterprise/
alex-stamos-security-facebookfive-minute-cio

Krebs, Brian, *Krebs on Security*, blog, undated. As of March 31, 2017:
https://krebsonsecurity.com

Lee, Robert M., "Critiques of the DHS/FBI's GRIZZLY STEPPE Report," blog post, December 30, 2016. As of March 31, 2017:
http://www.robertmlee.org/
critiques-of-the-dhsfbis-grizzly-steppe-report/

Lema, Karen, "Bangladesh Bank Heist Was 'State-Sponsored': U.S. Official," Reuters, March 29, 2017. As of March 31, 2017:
http://www.reuters.com/article/
us-cyber-heist-philippines-idUSKBN1700TI

Leyden, John, "Russia's to Blame for Pro-ISIS Megahack on French TV Network," *The Register*, June 10, 2015. As of March 31, 2017:
https://www.theregister.co.uk/2015/06/10/russian_trolls_staged_tv5monde_megahack_shocker/

Lin, Herbert, "Thoughts on Threat Assessment in Cyberspace," *I/S: A Journal of Law and Policy for the Information Society*, Vol. 8, No. 2, 2012, pp. 337–355.

———, "Attribution of Malicious Cyber Incidents: From Soup to Nuts," *Journal of International Affairs*, Winter 2016. As of March 31, 2017:
https://jia.sipa.columbia.edu/attribution-malicious-cyber-incidents

Mandiant, *APT1: Exposing One of China's Cyber Espionage Units*, 2013.

Markoff, John, and David E. Sanger, "In a Computer Worm, A Possible Biblical Tale," *New York Times*, September 29, 2010.

Matlack, Carol, Michael Riley, and Jordan Robertson, "The Company Securing Your Internet Has Close Ties to Russian Spies," *Bloomberg Businessweek*, March 19, 2015. As of March 31, 2017:
https://www.bloomberg.com/news/articles/2015-03-19/cybersecurity-kaspersky-has-close-ties-to-russian-spies

McLinn, James, "Major Power Outages in the U.S., and Around the World," in *IEEE Reliability Society 2009 Annual Technology Report*, 2009.

Morgan, Steve, "Cybersecurity Market Reaches $75 Billion in 2015; Expected to Reach $170 Billion by 2020," *Forbes*, December 20, 2015. As of March 31, 2017:
https://www.forbes.com/sites/stevemorgan/2015/12/20/cybersecurity%E2%80%8B-%E2%80%8Bmarket-reaches-75-billion-in-2015%E2%80%8B%E2%80%8B-%E2%80%8Bexpected-to-reach-170-billion-by-2020/#6d91f47e10c3

National Institute of Standards and Technology, *Managing Information Security Risk: Organization, Mission, and Information System View*, Special Publication 800-39, Gaithersburg, Md., March 2011. As of March 31, 2017:
http://nvlpubs.nist.gov/nistpubs/Legacy/SP/nistspecialpublication800-39.pdf

National Security Agency, "Signals Intelligence," web page, May 3, 2016. As of March 31, 2017:
https://www.nsa.gov/what-we-do/signals-intelligence/

Norton-Taylor, Richard, "Titan Rain: How Chinese Hackers Targeted Whitehall," *The Guardian*, September 4, 2007.

Novetta Threat Research Group, "Operation Blockbuster: Unravelling the Long Thread of the Sony Attack," web page, February 24, 2016. As of March 31, 2017:
http://www.novetta.com/2016/02/operation-blockbuster-unraveling-the-long-thread-of-the-sony-attack/

Owens, William A., Kenneth W. Dam, and Herbert S. Lin, eds., *Technology, Policy, Law, and Ethics Regarding U.S. Acquisition and Use of Cyberattack Capabilities*, Washington, D.C.: National Academies Press, 2009.

Paganini, Pierluigi, "FireEye Claims Russian APT28 Hacked France's TV5Monde Channel," *Security Affairs*, June 10, 2015. As of March 31, 2017:
http://securityaffairs.co/wordpress/37710/hacking/apt28-hacked-tv5monde.html

Perlroth, Nicole, and David E. Sanger, "Hackers Hit Dozens of Countries Exploiting Stolen NSA Tool," *New York Times*, May 12, 2017. As of May 25, 2017:
https://www.nytimes.com/2017/05/12/world/europe/uk-national-health-service-cyberattack.html

Polityuk, Pavel, "Ukraine to Probe Suspected Russian Cyber Attack on Grid," Reuters, December 31, 2015. As of March 31, 2017:
http://www.reuters.com/article/us-ukraine-crisis-malware-idUSKBN0UE0ZZ20151231

Rid, Thomas, and Ben Buchanan, "Attributing Cyber Attacks," *Journal of Strategic Studies*, Vol. 38, Nos. 1–2, 2015.

Rogers, Marc, "No, North Korea Didn't Hack Sony," *Daily Beast*, December 24, 2014. As of March 31, 2017:
http://www.thedailybeast.com/articles/2014/12/24/no-north-korea-didn-t-hack-sony

Sanger, David E., "Obama Order Sped Up Wave of Cyberattacks Against Iran," *New York Times*, June 1, 2012. As of May 24, 2017:
http://www.nytimes.com/2012/06/01/world/middleeast/obama-ordered-wave-of-cyberattacks-against-iran.html

Sanger, David E., and Martin Fackler, "NSA Breached North Korean Networks Before Sony Attack, Officials Say," *New York Times*, January 18, 2015. As of March 31, 2017:
https://www.nytimes.com/2015/01/19/world/asia/nsa-tapped-into-north-korean-networks-before-sony-attack-officials-say.html

Schmitt, Michael N., ed., *Tallinn Manual on the International Law Applicable to Cyber Warfare*, Cambridge, England: Cambridge University Press, 2013.

Schneier, Bruce, "Did North Korea Really Attack Sony?" *The Atlantic*, December 22, 2014. As of May 24, 2017:
https://www.theatlantic.com/international/archive/2014/12/did-north-korea-really-attack-sony/383973/

Segal, Adam, "The Continued Importance of the U.S.-China Cyber Dialogue," *Net Politics*, blog post, Council on Foreign Relations, January 23, 2017. As of March 31, 2017:
http://blogs.cfr.org/cyber/2017/01/23/the-continued-importance-of-the-u-s-china-cyber-dialogue/

Shachtman, Noah, "Russia's Top Cyber Sleuth Foils U.S. Spies, Helps Kremlin Pals," *Wired*, July 23, 2012. As of March 31, 2017:
https://www.wired.com/2012/07/ff_kaspersky/all/

Shevchenko, Sergei, and Adrian Nish, "Cyber Heist Attribution," *Threat Research*, BAE Systems blog, May 13, 2016. As of March 31, 2017:
http://baesystemsai.blogspot.com/2016/05/cyber-heist-attribution.html

Shodan, homepage, undated. As of March 31, 2017:
https://shodan.io

Smith, Brad, "The Need for a Digital Geneva Convention," *The Official Microsoft Blog*, February 14, 2017. As of March 31, 2017:
https://blogs.microsoft.com/on-the-issues/2017/02/14/need-digital-geneva-convention/#sm.0000lgk5vy1e5he6gzh99xggdxmu5

Soltra, homepage, undated. As of May 26, 2017:
https://www.soltra.com/en/

"Spelling Mistake Prevented Hackers Taking $1Bn in Bank Heist," Reuters via *The Guardian*, March 10, 2016. As of March 31, 2017:
https://www.theguardian.com/business/2016/mar/10/spelling-mistake-prevented-bank-heist

Sterling, Bruce, "The Project Grey Goose Cyberwar Report," *Wired*, August 3, 2009. As of May 12, 2017:
https://www.wired.com/2009/08/the-project-grey-goose-cyberwar-report/

Stoll, Clifford, *The Cuckoo's Egg*, New York: Doubleday, 2012.

Sulmeyer, Michael, and Amy Chang, "Three Observations on China's Approach to State Action in Cyberspace," *Lawfare*, blog post, January 22, 2017. As of March 31, 2017:
https://www.lawfareblog.com/three-observations-chinas-approach-state-action-cyberspace

Symantec Security Response, "'Forkmeiamfamous': Seaduke, Latest Weapon in the Duke Armory," blog post, July 13, 2015. As of March 31, 2017:
https://www.symantec.com/connect/blogs/
forkmeiamfamous-seaduke-latest-weapon-duke-armory

———, "SWIFT Attackers' Malware Linked to More Financial Attacks," blog post, May 26, 2016. As of March 31, 2017:
https://www.symantec.com/connect/blogs/
swift-attackers-malware-linked-more-financial-attacks

Thornburgh, Nathan, "The Invasion of the Chinese Cyberspies," *Time,* August 29, 2005.

"ThreatExchange Documentation," web page, Facebook for Developers, undated. As of May 26, 2017:
https://developers.facebook.com/docs/threat-exchange/v2.9

UN—*See* United Nations.

United Nations General Assembly, *Group of Governmental Experts on Developments in the Field of Information and Telecommunications in the Context of International Security,* Report No. A/70/174, July 22, 2015. As of March 31, 2017:
http://www.un.org/ga/search/view_doc.asp?symbol=A/70/174

U.S. Department of Defense, *The DoD Cyber Strategy,* Washington, D.C., April 2015.

U.S. Department of Homeland Security, *National Cyber Incident Response Plan,* Washington, D.C., December 2016. As of March 31, 2017:
https://www.us-cert.gov/sites/default/files/ncirp/
National_Cyber_Incident_Response_Plan.pdf

U.S. Department of Homeland Security and the Federal Bureau of Investigation, *GRIZZLY STEPPE—Russian Malicious Cyber Activity,* Joint Analysis Report, December 29, 2016. As of March 31, 2017:
https://www.us-cert.gov/sites/default/files/publications/
JAR_16-20296A_GRIZZLY%20STEPPE-2016-1229.pdf

U.S. Department of Homeland Security and Office of the Director of National Intelligence, "Joint Statement from the Department of Homeland Security and Office of the Director of National Intelligence on Election Security," October 7, 2016. As of March 31, 2017:
https://www.dhs.gov/news/2016/10/07/
joint-statement-department-homeland-security-and-office-
director-national

U.S. Department of Justice, "U.S. Charges Five Chinese Military Hackers for Cyber Espionage Against U.S. Corporations and a Labor Organization for Commercial Advantage," No. 14–528, May 19, 2014. As of March 31, 2017:
https://www.justice.gov/opa/pr/
us-charges-five-chinese-military-hackers-cyber-
espionage-against-us-corporations-and-labor

———, "Seven Iranians Working for Islamic Revolutionary Guard Corps-Affiliated Entities Charged for Conducting Coordinated Campaign of Cyber Attacks Against U.S. Financial Sector," March 24, 2016. As of March 31, 2017:
https://www.justice.gov/opa/pr/
seven-iranians-working-islamic-revolutionary-guard-corps-
affiliated-entities-charged

———, "U.S. Charges Russian FSB Officers and Their Criminal Conspirators for Hacking Yahoo and Millions of Email Accounts," March 15, 2017. As of March 31, 2017:
https://www.justice.gov/opa/pr/
us-charges-russian-fsb-officers-and-their-criminal-conspirators-
hacking-yahoo-and-millions

U.S. House of Representatives, "FISA Amendments Act of 2008," HR 6304, July 10, 2008. As of March 31, 2017:
https://www.congress.gov/bill/110th-congress/house-bill/6304

U.S. Office of the Director of National Intelligence, "Analytic Standards," Washington, D.C., Intelligence Community Directive 203, January 2, 2015. As of March 31, 2017:
https://www.dni.gov/files/documents/ICD/
ICD%20203%20Analytic%20Standards.pdf

———, "Assessing Russian Activities and Intentions in Recent U.S. Elections," Washington, D.C., Intelligence Community Assessment, January 6, 2017.

U.S. Senate, *Foreign Cyber Threats to the United States*, hearing before the Committee on Armed Services, Washington, D.C., January 5, 2017. As of March 31, 2017:
http://www.armed-services.senate.gov/hearings/
17-01-05-foreign-cyber-threats-to-the-united-states

U.S. Supreme Court, "Frequently Asked Questions—General Information" web page, undated. As of March 31, 2017:
https://www.supremecourt.gov/faq.aspx#faqgi9

Wilson, Kara, "In Case You Missed It: The FireEye Top Five Stories of the Week," *FireEye*, blog post, June 12, 2015. As of March 31, 2017:
https://www.fireeye.com/blog/executive-perspective/2015/06/
in_case_you_missedi0.html

Yadron, Danny, "When Cybersecurity Meets Geopolitics," *Wall Street Journal*, March 23, 2015. As of March 31, 2017:
http://blogs.wsj.com/digits/2015/03/23/
when-cybersecurity-meets-geopolitics/

YARA, "YARA in a Nutshell," web page, undated. As of March 31, 2017:
http://virustotal.github.io/yara/

Zetter, Kim, *Countdown to Zero Day: Stuxnet and the Launch of the World's First Digital Weapon*, New York: Crown, 2014a.

———, "The Evidence That North Korea Hacked Sony is Flimsy," *Wired*, December 17, 2014b. As of May 24, 2017:
https://www.wired.com/2014/12/
evidence-of-north-korea-hack-is-thin/

———, "That Insane, $81M Bangladesh Bank Heist? Here's What We Know," *Wired*, May 17, 2016. As of March 31, 2017:
https://www.wired.com/2016/05/
insane-81m-bangladesh-bank-heist-heres-know/